ADO KYROU

Luis Buñuel:

AN INTRODUCTION

TRANSLATED BY ADRIENNE FOULKE

SIMON AND SCHUSTER, NEW YORK, 1963

Library of Congress Catalog Card Number: 63-15366

Manufactured in the United States of America

CONTENTS

5

ACKNOWLEDGMENTS

We wish to thank the following for their kind permission to include selections from their writings or to reproduce photographs: Janine André-Bazin, Yvonne Baby, Fernande Lillette, Jacques F. Aranda, André Breton, Jacques B. Brunius, Oscar Dancigers, Jacques Doniol-Valcroze, François Gergely, Henry Miller, Octavio Paz, Michel Piccoli, Georges Sadoul and François Truffaut. We also gratefully acknowledge the cooperation of: *Cahiers du Cinéma, Cinéma 62, Positif;* Éditions du Cerf for permission to quote from the work of André Bazin; *Interspectacles* for permission to quote excerpts from the screenplay of *Viridiana;* the Library of the Institut des Hautes Études Cinématographiques; and the Cineldé, Columbia and Marceau-Cocinor film societies. Above all, we thank Luis Buñuel for his continued interest and help.

PROLOGUE

One evening in 1928 a group of surrealist artists gathered at the Ursulines Theater in Paris for a private screening of a recently completed film by Man Ray, *Le Mystère du Château de Dé*. Afterward, André Breton and the others were discussing it enthusiastically when the owner of the theater suggested that they stay another fifteen minutes to see a new film brought in the day before by two young Spaniards.

The film shown to Man Ray and his guests that night was *Un Chien Andalou*, the first work of Luis Buñuel, whose co-director was none other than Salvador Dali.

Buñuel was sitting behind the screen during the projection, nervously fingering some stones in his pocket while he waited to see how these men, whom he already thought of as old friends, would react. They were greatly impressed and immediately recognized Buñuel as one of them. That night Buñuel and his film joined forces with surrealism in the beginning of an important and complex relationship. At the same time, Buñuel's very special view of the world began to transform film. Spain and the dream, the suprareal and the magical, invaded the camera obscura.

At a time when experimental film-making was bogged down in pure abstraction, dry technique, and "depth" psychology, a Buñuel was needed.

Today he is needed more than ever.

Tomorrow he will be the basis of a cinema that is responsive to the essential changes which the space age has brought about in our physical, social, moral, and spiritual world.

But let's turn back the clock.

9

1.   BUÑUEL:

THE MAN AND HIS WORK

PREHISTORY

The Buñuel family comes from Calanda, a town in the Spanish province of Teruel.

Luis' grandfather was born and died in the nineteenth century. He was a farmer and had two sons. The elder, Joaquín, who became a pharmacist, died of cholera in 1908. His second son, Leonardo, survived the cholera epidemic and fathered seven children: Luis, born in 1900; Maria, in 1901, Alicia, in 1902; Conchita, in 1904; Leonardo, in 1907; Margarita, in 1912; and Alfonso, in 1915.

Luis' father was an interesting man; his eldest son inherited his intelligence, his love of justice and liberty, and his restlessness. Leonardo Buñuel had left home when he was fourteen to join the army. His adventurous spirit was gratified when he was sent to Cuba to fight against the United States. He rose to the rank of captain. After the war he settled in Cuba, where he set himself up in business selling ironware. Two of his employees, Casteleiro and Vizoso, later became his partners. Today these two names represent one of the richest business firms in Central America.

In 1899 Leonardo returned to Spain for a visit. He met a seventeen-year-old girl in Calanda and fell in love with her. At the time he was forty-two. Their marriage took place shortly afterward and the couple returned to Cuba. In 1914, the Buñuels went back to Calanda for good. They bought property there and became involved with the management of their fairly large holdings. Leonardo died in 1923. Local people remember him as a cultured, sociable man with high ideals. Although he was a man of property, his social ideas were quite advanced, and he was a friend of

the group that founded the liberal newspaper of Saragossa, *El Heraldo de Aragón.*

Luis Buñuel always speaks affectionately of his mother. Born in 1882, she was, and still is, very beautiful. She comes from a family named Portolés, which, in the eighteenth century, split into two branches, one living in upper Aragón (Huesca) and the other in lower Aragón. Buñuel's mother belongs to the latter branch. She has the characteristics of her family: nobility of spirit, elegance, distinction, intelligence. Her son says that she has "genius."

LUIS

People who like to spread confusion because they themselves are either confused or malicious have written a great deal of nonsense about Buñuel. It has been claimed, for example, that he dines on ants. Other people pretend not to know that sadism meaning admiration for the works of the great de Sade and sympathy with the revolutionary ideas of that perpetual prisoner, and sadism as the word is used in the tabloids are not one and the same thing.

Luis was a normal child—"pathologically normal," as an American psychoanalyst might put it. Very clean and meticulous, he always kept his things in exemplary order. He was a good, studious pupil who had no troubles in school except when, out of sheer perversity, he refused to wear the hat prescribed by the Jesuit secondary school he attended.

Luis' Jesuit education made a lasting impression on him. Buñuel has said that he was struck by the way the Jesuits channeled the sexual urges of their young charges by leading them to be actually (physically) in love with the Virgin Mary. Thus the boys masturbated in front of plaster statues of the Mother of Christ and did not think of chasing flesh-and-blood girls.

Any child brought up by priests bears some trace of this upbringing. With normal boys, religious education is transformed in time into a healthy reaction *against.* Buñuel was a normal boy.

Blasphemy, provocation, and scandal constituted a joyous world

in which young Luis felt as much at home as a lover in moonlight. He would often say mock masses, dressing up in religious costumes, much to the delight of his little sisters. The girls admired their handsome big brother and lent themselves to all his schemes, no matter how outlandish these might seem to adults. Next to the magic lantern, the Buñuel children liked weird competitions best. One day they would see who could drink the most vinegar and sugar, the next, who would dare eat cigarette stubs picked up in the street, or sandwiches full of ants. The mastermind of these childhood rites certainly did not eat ants regularly. It *is* true that he was a vegetarian from the age of eighteen to twenty, that he sang in the church choir in Calanda, and, above all, that he was irresistibly attracted to the opposite sex from a very early age. As a child, he stole his sisters' toys to give to little girls whom he wanted to dazzle.

Luis' childhood was in the image of his films—a thunderous roll of drums, resounding with anguish and savagery, hope and despair. The drum that plays so important a musical part in his films figured in what was for Luis, as a child, the most exciting of holidays. Once a year, during the Easter season, all the drummers of the town poured into the streets. For four days their ceaseless beating accompanied the religious ceremonies, the processions, and the epic, drunken brawls. For four days and three nights, the drums heralded the end of one world or the beginning of another world, another life—as, at the circus, the drums announce a great acrobatic act. Buñuel responded to the summons of those drums with an irresistible impulse to fling himself into the void.

He went to the University of Madrid, and there, at the Residencia de Estudiantes, he became a friend of Dali and García Lorca and met José Ortega y Gasset, Ramón Gómez de la Serna, and the poet Rafael Alberti. He founded the first Spanish film club. From 1920 to 1923 he added film screenings to the activities of the Residencia.

PARIS

In 1925, Buñuel went to Paris, ostensibly to work with the International Institute of Intellectual Co-operation, but actually, he concentrated on making a place for himself in film circles.

Ever since *Los Olvidados* (*The Young and the Damned* in the United States) was shown at the Cannes Festival in 1951, brochures, articles, and slim little books have analyzed the most insignificant historical facts of the life, multiple adventures and misadventures of Buñuel. I prefer to stick to the main lines and skip the spicy intimate tidbits. In this book you will find a series of critiques of the films which, taken together, reveal a man.

Briefly then:

Buñuel saw Lang's *Les Trois Lumières* at the Vieux Colombier. It was a revelation. He must make films.

He read Jean Epstein's critical pieces in *L'Esprit Nouveau*.

He became the nineteenth pupil of the Académie du Cinéma, which was directed by Camille Bardoux, Alex Allain, and Jean Epstein. The other eighteen pupils were all White Russians.

Thanks to the Académie, he worked as an apprentice on Epstein's *Mauprat* and *La Chute de la Maison Usher* (*The Fall of the House of Usher*).

The cameraman Duverger got him a job as assistant on *La Sirène des Tropiques,* directed by those great specialists of the art film, Etiévant and Mario Nalpas.

He followed, from a distance, what André Breton and the other surrealists whom he so much admired were doing.

Gómez de la Serna suggested a scenario on the order of Alberto Cavalcanti's *Rien que des Heures.* It was to be a short film that described the production of a newspaper and, at the same time, brought the whole paper to life from front page to back: politics, crimes, church news, society column, and so on.

On one of his return visits to Spain, Buñuel's mother gave him a hundred and thirty-five thousand francs to make his own film.

Luis Buñuel, artilleryman,
1921

Luis Buñuel in 1955 with his
portrait by Salvador Dali
(painted in 1923)

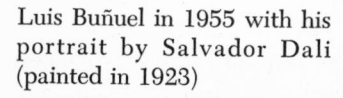

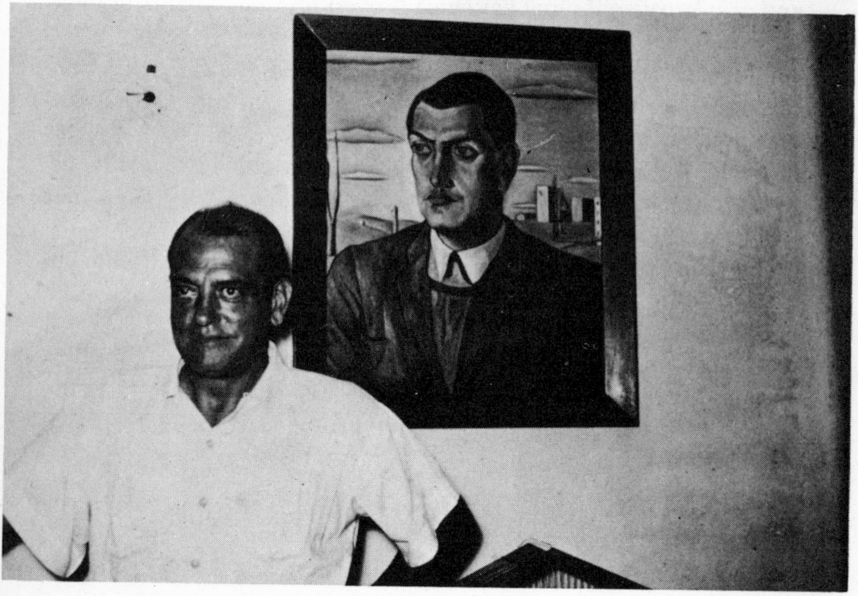

Back in Paris, he dropped the idea of the film about the newspaper and spent his mother's money in night clubs.

He wrote poems and other works that he wished to have published under the title *Un Chien Andalou*. ("A Giraffe," first published in *Le Surréalisme au Service de la Révolution,* and reproduced here on page 134, is a part of this group.)

He received a telegram from Dali: "Come to Cadaques." He went. The two friends lazed away the days. Dali dreamed of ants.

Buñuel returned to Paris. He had quarreled irreparably with Epstein when he told the master how little he thought of director Abel Gance. He began to make the film *Un Chien Andalou.*

UN CHIEN ANDALOU

Buñuel's first film (made in 1928) unquestionably marks an important date in the history of the cinema, but it does not seem to me comparably significant so far as Buñuel himself is concerned. This is because Dali's role in the work is as large as it is debatable, and also because Buñuel has since proved himself capable of making much less "abstract" films.

To be more explicit: *Un Chien Andalou* is one film, probably the only one, that is a doctrinaire expression of automatism. Automatism is valuable when it serves to free the self. When it hides the self, albeit under sometimes brilliant fustian, it is superfluous. *Un Chien Andalou* is a forced film, unlike others by Buñuel that flow in a continuous, unchecked stream from the self.

Dali dreams of ants. He tells his dreams to Buñuel, who, in turn, recounts his own dreams. Why, the two friends ask each other, not make a film from these dreams?

In three days they wrote the scenario of *Un Chien Andalou.** As they conceived it, the film consisted of a series of gags. They deliberately eliminated any gag that could—at least in their opinion —be rationally explained.

* The scenario is on page 142.

Buñuel went back to Paris and filmed the script in two weeks. Dali went to Paris just in time for the last day's shooting.

Everyone interested in cinema—or nearly everyone—now knows this work. Rather than analyze it sentence by sentence, let us ask whether Buñuel and Dali succeeded in their search for the irrational—and what was the public's reaction to the *scandale* they were so eager to bring off.

I am convinced that Buñuel and Dali were aiming at different things. Buñuel sought to catch a glimpse of that incandescent world in which dream and reality mingle in a magnificent gesture of liberation; Dali hoped to shock the bourgeoisie. Between Buñuel and the great self-publicist, the abyss of sincerity opens wide.

Everything that today seems to us facile or superficially surrealist, everything that recalls the dream sequence Dali worked out much later for Hitchcock's film *Spellbound,* everything that is merely symbolism (Batcheff's conversation with his double, schoolbooks turning into revolvers), is certainly attributable to Dali.

Other sequences are real cries of revolt. When the dream is used not as a Freudian study but as an expression of human anguish, that is when the voice of Buñuel speaks. Take a single example: From a window a couple witnesses an accident in the street; they are helpless to intervene. Immediately after the accident they indulge in dreamlike erotic play. There is no room here for the "beautiful dream," for aestheticism, for deceit; it is a question of catching latent life, of crying out in anguish and love, of forcing us to take cognizance of a macabre humor. In such sequences, in which Buñuel's hand is apparent, the irrational makes its triumphal entry. But Buñuel's irrational, while it foreshadows the highly original sequences in *L'Age d'Or,* is adulterated by the sophisticated shock effects Dal strives for.

Since 1929, when *Un Chien Andalou* was first shown, it has been a recognized classic in art film theaters and societies. The amateur viewer-analysts dissect it as if it were a dream sequence in a psychological film.

In turning to the cinema, Buñuel had not wanted to make an attractive film but rather one that *embarrassed.* That is why he

opens the film with an unbearable scene: ". . . The razor blade passes over the young girl's eyeball, sectioning it." For the first time in the history of the cinema, a director tries not to please but rather to alienate nearly all potential spectators.

Though some stupid and ill-informed critics despatched Buñuel to limbo, the snobbish, *avant-garde* section of the public appropriated *Un Chien Andalou*. It was the talk of the smart set, and Buñuel (who, in *La Révolution surréaliste*, No. 12, had violently denounced "the pack of imbeciles who found beauty or poetry in what is, in essence, nothing less than a desperate, passionate appeal to murder") came to see that scandal for scandal's sake—gratuitous shock, that is—upset no one.

His second film, *L'Age d'Or*, did not permit any abstract interpretations. It was not a film the middle class could stomach. *L'Age d'Or* was poison.

L'AGE D'OR

With *L'Age d'Or*, Luis Buñuel, surrealist, began a new era of film making. Actually, despite the reservations mentioned earlier, *Un Chien Andalou*, too, had been revolutionary.

On the eve of the talking picture, the break between popular cinema and the art film was already complete. The aesthetes (I use the word in its pejorative sense, although a certain aesthetic standard is always necessary) had carried the day in France. They had succeeded in making the abstract prevail.

Ballets of every kind were the rage: ballets of gypsy fairs, ballets with cubist décors, ballets about casseroles, and so on. Lights, kitchen utensils, etc., reigned supreme. The aesthetic film had banished the gag, and the colander had supplanted man. The redoubtable impressionists, or, better still, *avant-gardists* (they well deserve the military term), were working at turning the cinema into a field of maneuvers from which man was definitely excluded. Man Ray and a few Dadaists went to such maniacal extremes that they were defeated by their own excesses. A return to emotion was needed to keep the cinema from sinking into the mire in

which so-called modern painting and music—as some conceive modern—find themselves at present.

Buñuel (or surrealism) is a pivot about which the cinema can veer toward genuinely felt emotion. Such a trend began with *Un Chien Andalou* and took definite form with *L'Age d'Or*.

Until 1928 the film had dealt with both reality and the dream. But it was a hobbling kind of reality because the film makers forgot to include in it certain essential elements such as imagination, and the dream was even more distorted because they forgot that it has no vigor or value unless it is rooted in reality.

For Buñuel dream is not necessarily Freudian; it is no longer set apart from the day-to-day; dream *is*. In a word, it is a matter of realism, of reality that contains surrealism just as surrealism contains reality. The images in *L'Age d'Or* are an exact reproduction of what the eye, rinsed clear of the film of habit, can behold. After de Chirico, Max Ernst, and a few other painters, Buñuel, by means of the cinema—richer than painting because it is at one and the same time movement, association, detail, and ensemble—gives us back the "savage eye" of which Breton speaks in *Le Surréalisme et la Peinture*.

With his second film Buñuel achieved perfection in free cinematic expression. Initially it was called *La Bête Andalouse* and was conceived as a sequel to *Un Chien Andalou*. In fact, Buñuel and Dali had decided to do a second film based on the gags they had not used in *Un Chien Andalou*.

Buñuel went to Spain to work with Dali, but they had only one joint work session. The two men had already grown apart. Buñuel did not recognize his friend. *L'Age d'Or* is a film by Buñuel *without* Dali, and if the latter's name still appears among the credits, it is thanks to the courtesy of Buñuel. He used only one of Dali's gags in the picture—the gentleman strolling with a stone on his head.

Dali himself wrote, in *The Secret Life of Salvador Dali*: "My idea was that the film should express the violence of the love that is impregnated by the splendid creations of Catholic myths. . . . Buñuel was filming *L'Age d'Or* alone, and I was virtually cut off. . . . Buñuel had just finished *L'Age d'Or*. I was frightfully dis-

appointed. The film was only a caricature of my ideas. Catholicism was attacked in a primitive, quite unpoetic way. . . ."

Let us, then, forget Dali and get back to Buñuel's film.

A documentary-like opening announces that the film is an account of fact, a reportage, rather than a fictionalized story or a work of the imagination. The first subtitle reads: "The scorpion belongs to the branch of the spider family that generally lives under stones."

The insipid music that accompanies this prologue underlines the absolute surrealism of what people like to call a "slice of life." In the same region, and as real as the scorpions, live a band of wretched, grotesque, horrible ruffians, the last survivors of a vanished age. Armed with rusty swords, pitchforks, and stout pieces of wood, these exhausted, moribund creatures draw on their last ounce of courage as they wait to do battle with the Majorcans. The Majorcans land after sending some archbishops as a vanguard. Victorious without having had to fight, they found Imperial Rome on this earth—the same earth that eventually absorbs the corpses of its former occupants.

While the governor officially lays the first stone of the new age, Buñuel's major theme bursts upon us: an admirable and unique call to love. Disregarding the ceremony, "a man and woman in fiercely lascivious embrace roll in the mud." Their mating cries drown out the governor's inaugural address. Throughout the rest of the film this intense love tears the prejudices, inhibitions, and laws of society to shreds. The passage from love to revolt is accomplished without harm to the lovers, however, for love is in itself revolt and kills only its enemies—those who harass love and deny life, the jackals of worldly wisdom who turn the left cheek. There are two camps: the lovers and the others. The very structure of a putrifying society makes it inevitable that they stand opposed. Society, outraged and terrified by love, with the dagger thrust deep in its side, mobilizes all its poison-spewing forces— its high functionaries, its priests, its families, its big words, its police, its sophisticates. The lovers, torn apart as one separates dogs in the street, each dragged to his daily dungeon, will not be

separated. Their love, their hatred, form chains that are inde-
structible.

Un Chien Andalou is, with the exception of a few sequences,
little more than filmed poetry. *L'Age d'Or*, is a film—a film that has
assimilated all cinematic tradition and speaks the true language
of the film. By this time, the cinema had opened increasingly wide
and deep vistas. The grammar of cinematography had been established by Griffith, Ince, Eisenstein, and a few others. Now
Buñuel forgot all the rules and created a great cinematic evoca-
tion of mad love. To do so, he needed to devise an infinitely richer
language than any hitherto available. Furthermore, he scorned
the technical strait jacket that hampered so many directors. He
became, in brief, an innovator on every level.

His great subject demanded that all boundaries be abolished,
in order to express fully the two most magnetic words in any language: love and revolt. The cinematic revolution was total.
Since then, the film has been able to express everything. *L'Age
d'Or* revealed it to itself.

Until *L'Age d'Or*, movie makers had not made use of repetition
to hyphenate diverse themes. With Buñuel, these repeated images
are so many leitmotivs that maintain the unity of dream and reality. Thus a woman's hair becomes a link between a poster that
Gaston Modot sees in a hairdresser's window and Lya Lys
stretched out on a divan. In the screenplay, Buñuel underlines this
sequence, saying that it "must give a coincidental reality to the
image the suspect has of her and reveal what, in fact, the young
girl was feeling or doing at the moment the character was looking at her."

Another image that returns often is that of fingers in motion—
for example, at various times the ring finger trembles on some object. "The effect of this nervous movement will be extremely disturbing since its significance is clearly masturbatory," he wrote
in the shooting script. A hand on a poster, the father's hand on a
bottle of iodine, the hand of the valet wiping a bottle, and, especially, the ringed finger of Lya Lys—all these images form a
bond between imagination and everyday actions. Similarly, erotic
desire is always expressed in the same way, i.e., teeth biting the

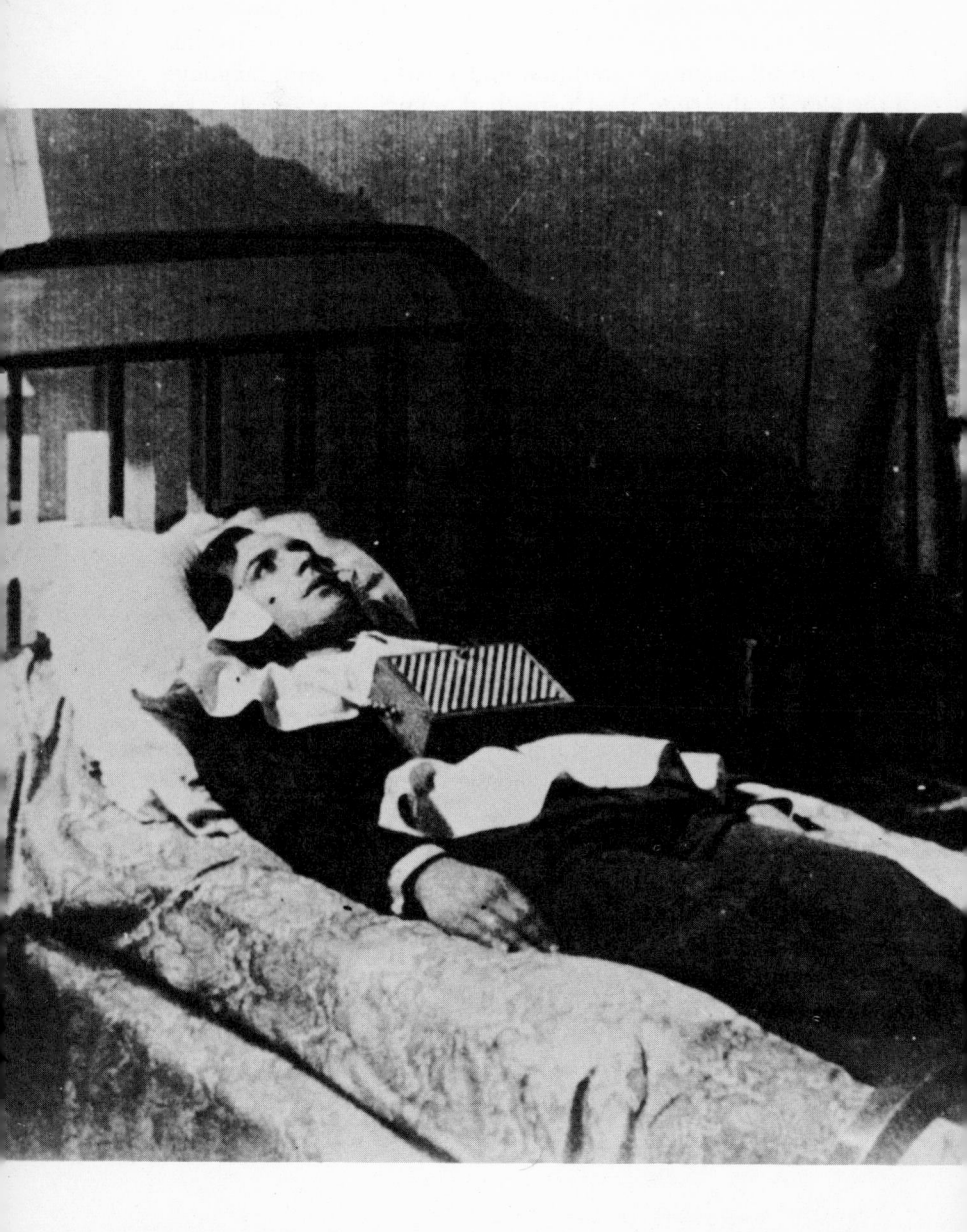

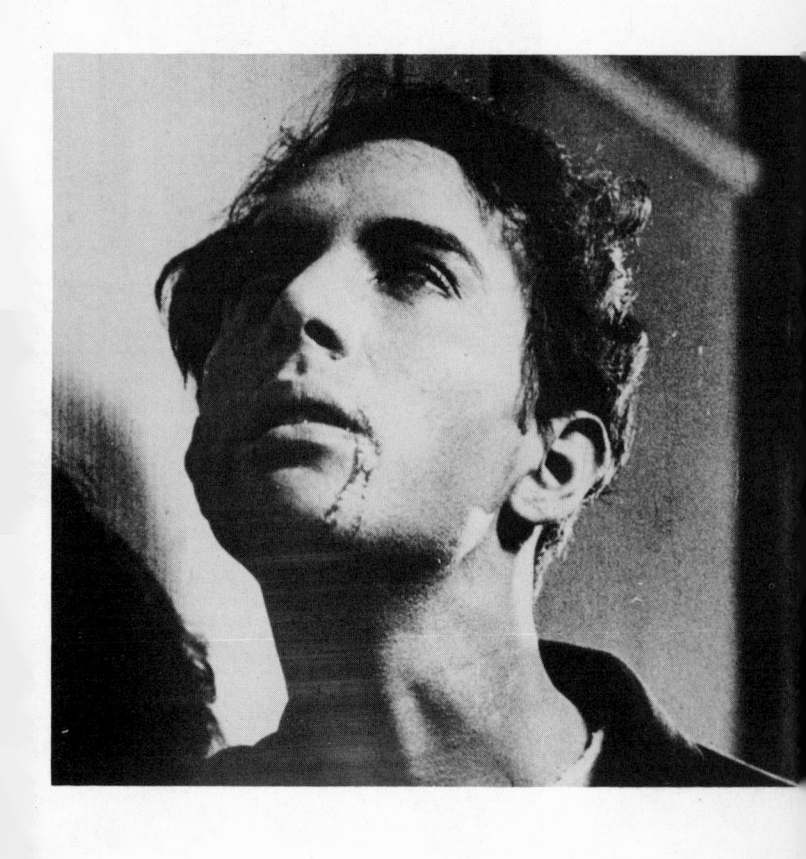

Pierre Batcheff in scenes from *Un Chien Andalou*

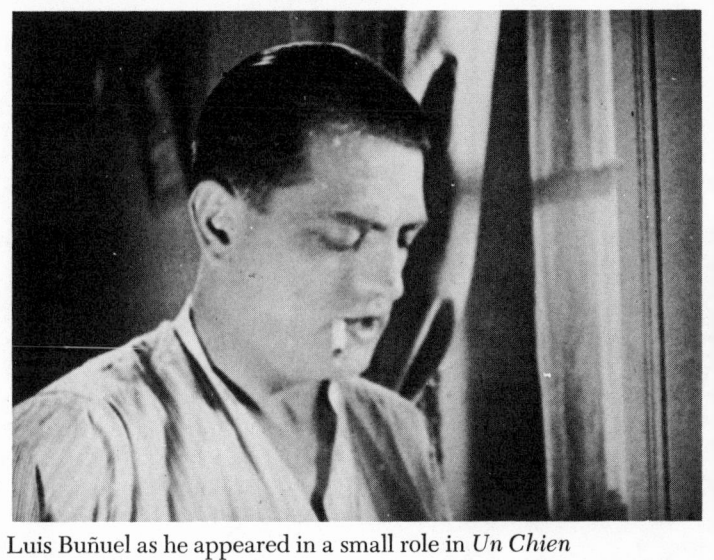

Luis Buñuel as he appeared in a small role in *Un Chien Andalou*

Another scene from *Un Chien Andalou*

lower lip. These details may pass unnoticed, but they are needed because they help create an atmosphere of total life.

The most perfect example of the meeting of cinema and surrealism is the mirror sequence, which I think is the most magnificently poetic sequence in the history of the film. When Lya Lys enters her bedroom and finds a cow on her bed, the animal's bell becomes the predominant sound, a sound which persists even after the cow disappears. In the next frame, we find Gaston Modot with the police, but the sound of the bell still persists, with the barking of dogs superimposed on it. As soon as we return to Lya Lys, who is leaning over her mirror, which reflects a sky with drifting clouds, the dual sound of bell and barking is enriched by the sound of the wind. This triple sound accompanies the lovers during the entire sequence, although they are miles apart. The two sounds—bell and barking—inform the spectator immediately that he is witnessing the union of two people whom distance does not separate. The wind hails the triumph of their union.

Let us not forget that *L'Age d'Or* is one of the first talking films, and that its sound effects have no technical function: they *are* the film. No one notices the "technique" of *L'Age d'Or*, which is one more argument in favor of the film's great value; it has so assimilated its own techniques as to make that technique, perfect as it is, disappear completely in the final result.

Dozens of articles have been written on the device of the interior monologues. In *L'Age d'Or*, the interior monologue, used in films for the first time, is not a trick but a primary element expressing the latent content of life.

The two lovers, revealed to themselves by love, desperately defend their union by declaring war on society, their weapons being indifference, scorn, and hatred. A man blinded in the war who might delay their meeting by so much as a moment is an enemy; an old woman, especially if she is the mother of the young girl, is slapped when her chatter separates the lovers. Love knows no *savoir-vivre* because it *is* life, and it slaps and kicks and precipitates catastrophes which lead society toward its total and desirable destruction.

But personal difficulties arise to threaten the couple, and thus

we reach the noteworthy love-torture sequence in the park. Under the influence of the place, which is hostile, inhibitions, snap judgments, atavisms raise their ghostly heads. It is then that the interior monologue (or, rather, dialogue) takes place. Lya Lys and Modot, who cannot make love in the park, eliminate the place and, when we see their closed mouths, we hear: "I'm cold." "Put out the light." "No, leave it on." And a little later: "Are you sleepy?" "I want to go to sleep." "Put your head here." "The pillow is nearer." "Where is your hand?" and so on, until we come to the exultant repetition of the two words "My love, my love, my love, my love, my love . . ." Their expressions exactly mirror the words they are saying without opening their lips. They do not think, they do not imagine that they are elsewhere, where they can make love without constraint: they *are* elsewhere. Place is vanquished, and not only place but time, too, for suddenly Lya Lys, as seen by Modot, ages twenty years, although she does not change her attitude or expression. Thus it is not only a question of the interior-monologue technique, as our current fancy film cutters understand it—which would have only a scant historical value—but rather of reality made present by sound, reality that knows how to cause two characters to make a marvelous, motionless but *real* leap into space and time, to a point where they may love each other.

Confronted with this exacerbated will to love, society is shocked and scandalized and tries in every way to defend itself. Never has a portrait of society been offered us in more penetrating and implacable colors. Without mentioning all the details that expose this riffraff, let us confine ourselves to the major scene of the reception. It is worth noting that this sort of reception has been used by some of our greatest film makers to expose and denounce the hypocrisy, baseness, and cowardice of the upper classes. Chaplin was the first, in one of Mack Sennett's best comedies, *Tillie's Punctured Romance* (1914). He fired a revolver and spread panic in the midst of a social evening complete with dancing. Inkijinov, Pudovkin's hero in *Storm Over Asia* (1928), becomes aware of his revolutionary future during an official ceremony, which he interrupts with a magnificent explosion of revolt.

Pabst, in *Pandora's Box* (1928), chooses a formal reception to loose a painfully sordid and hysterical drama in the midst of the strait-laced politeness of the guests. And who does not remember the extraordinary ballet-chase in Jean Renoir's *Rules of the Game* (1939), in which, linking burlesque and tragedy, he punctuates his healthfully destructive action with howls of terror and revolver shots while the poker-faced, genteel onlookers believe or pretend to believe that the spectacle was planned that way. In each of these instances, the slogan of society is the same: "Don't upset the established order."

To notice the cart on which the workers drink red wine would mean losing face for the characters in *L'Age d'Or*. Similarly, complete indifference greets the fire that breaks out in the kitchen of the big house and endangers the servants' lives. The case of the father who kills his son in cold blood is taken somewhat more seriously by the upper crust. But the murderer explains that the son had dared tear the cigarette he was rolling and thus deserved to die. The questionable explanation is unanimously accepted as only just, everyone breathes freely, and the party continues. These incidents serve to underline the outraged and violent reactions of the middle-class characters when they are ready to lynch a young man who had, with reason, slapped an ignoble old woman because she was an obstacle to love. The wretched cart can pass; they shut their eyes. The fire can break out in the kitchen, since that is a part of the house unknown to them. But love threatens them personally. It is the great enemy that can make the workers on the cart, the denizens of the kitchen, and the murdered boy rise against them.

Love will be defeated briefly by the lovers themselves, who are not yet masters of their inhibitions. Shaken by despair, the bearded orchestra leader leaves his podium and separates the couple. This character is society's last and most efficacious weapon. During this sequence the camera changes, not for reasons of technique but in response to a demand inherent in the dramatic evolution of the action, and it takes the place now of the orchestra leader, now of Lya Lys. Modot is for the moment unable to destroy this new *loveless* couple that is formed. He suffers to the ac-

companiment of an interminable roll of drums, and his reactions can only lead him to renewed revolt. In a fury, he throws objects —the symbols of his servitude—out the window, while at that very moment the survivors emerge from de Selligny's Château—the inevitable conclusion to what has taken place (*The 120 Days of Sodom*, by de Sade).

This final sequence is most enigmatic when considered in relation to the love story of Lya Lys and Modot. I believe that Buñuel wished to acknowledge the importance of de Sade's work, in which love must find renewed strength if it is to triumph over itself, that is, over its inhibitions. Only then will it become the great liberator.

It is clear that this sequence is also the apotheosis of the great battle against religion waged in *L'Age d'Or*. In aiming at this target, Buñuel knew that, as Karl Marx said, "criticism of Heaven is transformed into criticism of earth, criticism of religion into criticism of law, criticism of theology into criticism of politics." From the film's inception, the union of army and clergy is underlined in various ways: by the archbishops who come to colonize; by the monstrance that the reception guests bring with them; by the extraordinary description of "Imperial Rome, the secular seat of the Church," where "sometimes on Sundays" houses collapse as the Pope is celebrating Mass; by the Mariolater violinist. It is worth pointing out that in the scenario (see synopsis on page 149), before shooting began, the Château de Selligny scene was conceived differently. The survivors of "the most bestial of orgies" represented by their costumes and general appearance the major religions: the Duc de Blangis wears a mustache and beard, and is dressed like the Hebrews of the first century A.D.; President Curval is dressed like a lower-class Arab—sixth century A.D.; the Bishop of K., who enters limping, is dressed like a priest of the sixteenth century. In the scenario the Duc de Blangis, who "is clearly Jesus Christ," alone manages to survive the carnage, while in the actual filming the Bishop of K. takes over this task before he has lost his beard—which turns up again in the epilogue, together with some hair on a cross, snow-covered and beaten by the wind to the accompaniment of a two-step.

In any case, the meaning of this sequence is the same, for Jesus Christ perfectly represents the spirit of religiosity and mysticism.

If religion has been harshly dealt with, other pillars of middle-class domination have not been handled with kid gloves, either. Buñuel has given the police, the family, and the army the most vigorous blows they have ever received on the screen. Thus love stands forth alone as the great and unique hope, the major revolt of man.

L'AGE D'OR CREATES A SCANDAL

In February 1930, Eisenstein's film *The General Line* (also known as *The Old and the New*) was banned. The *L'Age d'Or* scandal broke the same year. From October 2 to December 3, the film, which had been duly passed by the censors, was shown without incident at Studio 28.* On the evening of October 3, a group of people attending the showing waited for the right moment to show their "superior intellectuality." On the screen, at the moment when a character places a monstrance in a stream, there were cries of "We'll see if there are still any Christians in France!" and "Down with the Jews!" Stink bombs exploded, spectators were man-handled, the screen was splashed with purple ink, seats were torn up, and pictures by Dali, Max Ernst, Man Ray, Miró, and Tanguy which were hanging in the theater lobby were slashed. After interrupting the showing and cutting the theater's telephone wires, the demonstrators—representatives of the Patriots' League and of the Anti-Jewish League—fled. But stink bombs, when weighed against a Buñuel film, amounted to no more than senile hysteria, and the performance was resumed.

The screen that bore this mark of "Christian illiteracy" should have been preserved so that *L'Age d'Or* could always have been run on it. Then the priests, the Fascists, the anti-Semites, and the superpatriots would have recognized themselves even more easily

---

* A commercial film theater in Montmartre whose name stems from the fact that it was founded in 1928.

in the parents of Lya Lys as well as in the governor, the Mario-laters, the politicos, and the Christ of the film.

The next day, the right-wing papers featured the incident, demanding that the most stringent measures be taken against the film. The Patriots' League released a statement protesting against the "immorality of this Bolshevik film," implying that an indignant public had caused the outbreak. A city official, M. the Provost de Launay, went to police headquarters and had a long talk with the director of censorship. He had already written the prefect of police, requesting that measures be taken against the "offal" of surrealism. His open letter had appeared in the papers on November 10. It contained the following splendid example of unconscious humor: the gentleman wished to take this opportunity to protest against "other films imported from or originating in Germany which are being or are to be shown in the Champs-Élysées quarter, only *two steps* from the tomb of the Unknown Soldier."

On December 5, following de Launay's intervention with the censorship authorities, the bureau asked the management of Studio 28 to suppress "two passages dealing with bishops." The cuts were made and the screenings continued normally.

On December 7, the grand campaign of the right-wing press advocating Fascist action against "subversive" films began. The campaign was spearheaded by *Le Figaro* and *L'Ami du Peuple*. Richard-Pierre Bodin wrote in *Le Figaro* of December 7:

"A film called *L'Age d'Or*—in which I defy any qualified authority to detect the slightest artistic merit—multiplies (in public showings!) its crop of utterly obscene, repugnant, and tawdry episodes. Country, family, religion are dragged through the mire. All those who saved the grandeur of France, all those who cherish the family and the innocence of childhood, all those who have faith in the future of a race which has enlightened the whole world, all those Frenchmen who have been chosen to protect you against the poison of rotten entertainment, now ask what you think of the job our censorship is doing. . . ."

On December 8, police headquarters asked that a line in the program notes be cut: "The Duc de Blangis is clearly Jesus Christ." On the 9th, M. Mauclaire, the manager of Studio 28, was

informed that a special censorship commission would review the film on the morning of the 11th. On the 10th, the morning papers received a release stating that *L'Age d'Or* was definitely banned. M. Mauclaire was so informed the same day at five-thirty in the afternoon. On the 10th, too, new articles appeared in the reactionary press.

"Let us say straight off that this production is boring. . . . This pretentious and dreary pensum has nothing to do with *avant-garde* art or with just plain art. The technical execution is so poor that it would elicit catcalls in the poorest film houses of our most provincial towns" (G. M., *Echo de Paris*, December 10, 1930). "This is a Bolshevik endeavor of a special, yes, of a truly special kind, which aims to corrupt us. Lenin's propaganda has found in certain more or less fly-by-night studios unexpected co-operation, and knows how to make use of it. . . ." (Gaëtan Sanvoisin, *Le Figaro*, December 10, 1930.)

The film was officially banned on December 11, and on the 12th, all copies were seized by the police. Here is the statement issued by police headquarters:

"In consequence of evidence verified this morning by the official commission that undertook to examine this film, shown in a theater in the Montmartre area, the prefect of police has brought charges against the manager of the theater. He will be prosecuted for an infraction of the decree of February 18, 1928, under the terms of which he may be fined up to five hundred francs and his establishment temporarily closed."

It should be noted that the damages caused by the superpatriots amounted to eight thousand francs.

Meanwhile, the Italian ambassador to France was so upset that, it seems, he remonstrated with the French government (he may have recognized his own sovereigns in the governor of the film and his wife).

The left-wing press came vigorously to the defense of *L'Age d'Or*. Especially noteworthy were the interesting appraisals by Roger Lesbats in *Le Populaire*, Lucie Derain in *Le Quotidien*, and Léon Mousinac in *L'Humanité*.

The surrealists published "A Questionnaire," in which they

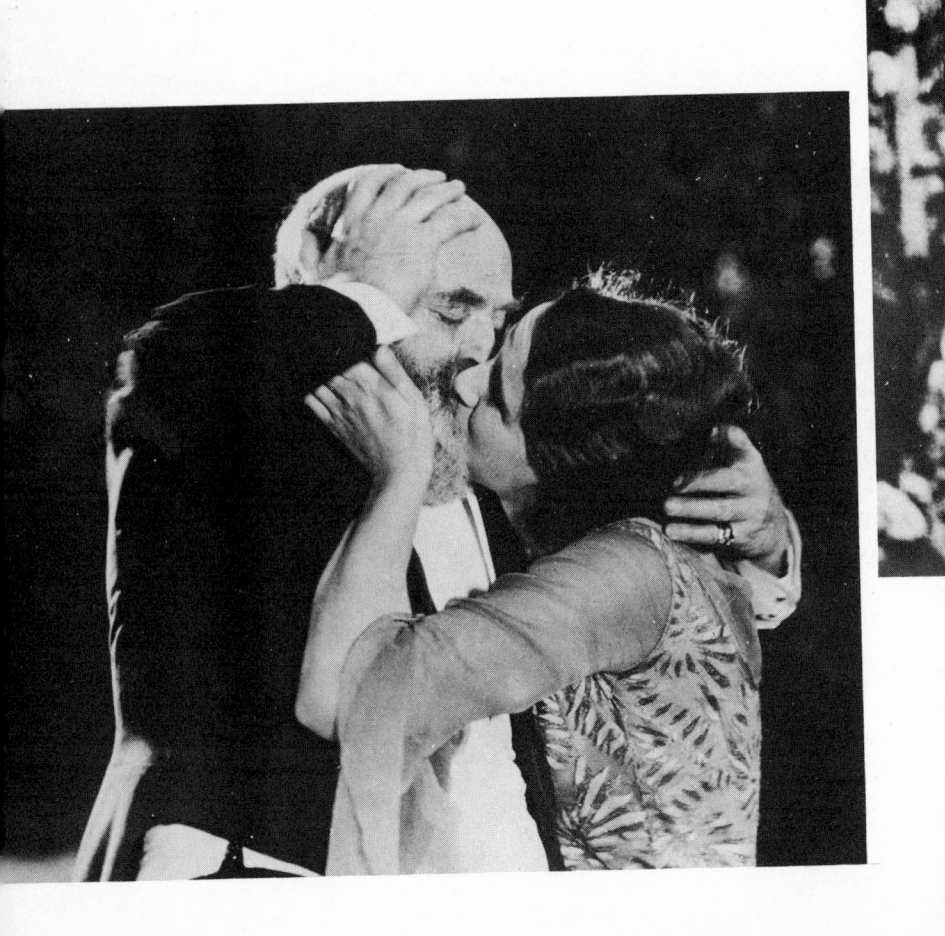

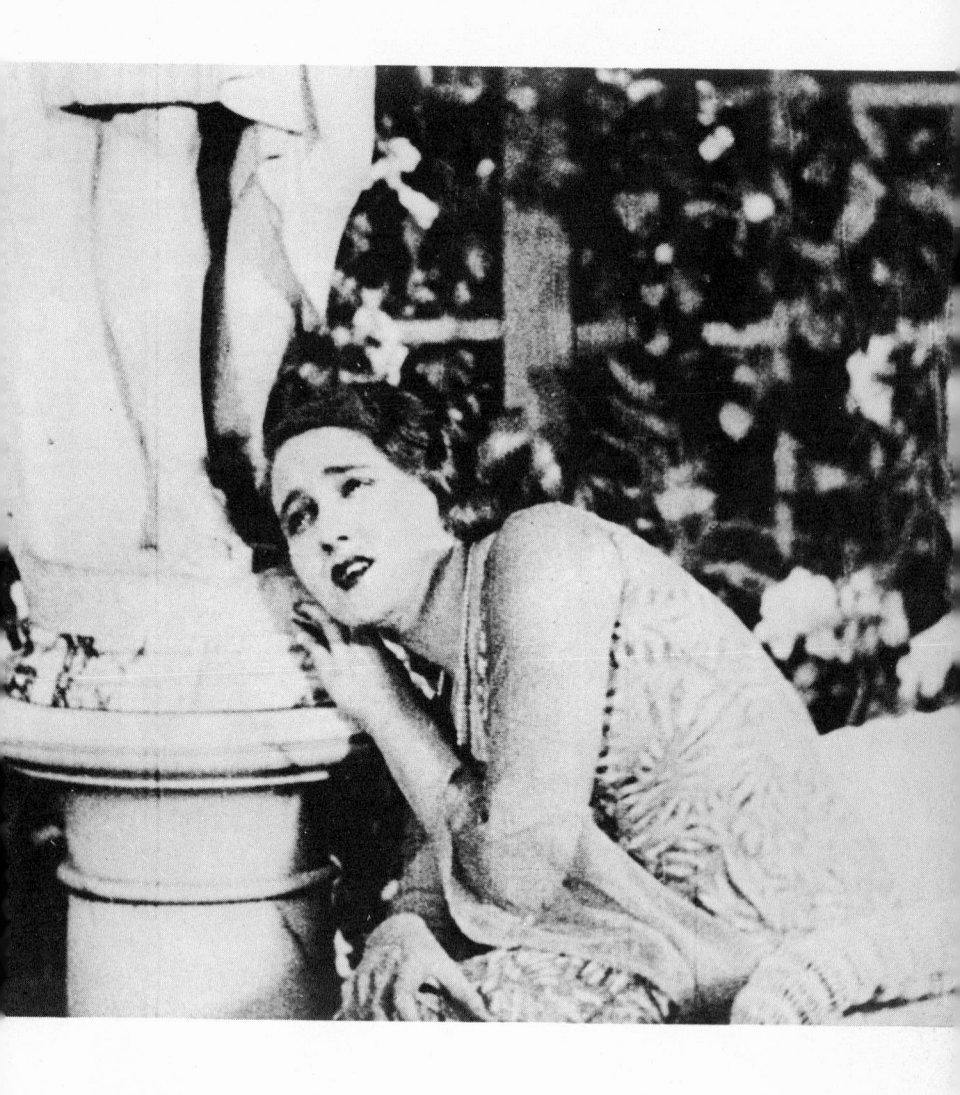

Gaston Modot and Lya Lys in scenes from *L'Age d'Or*

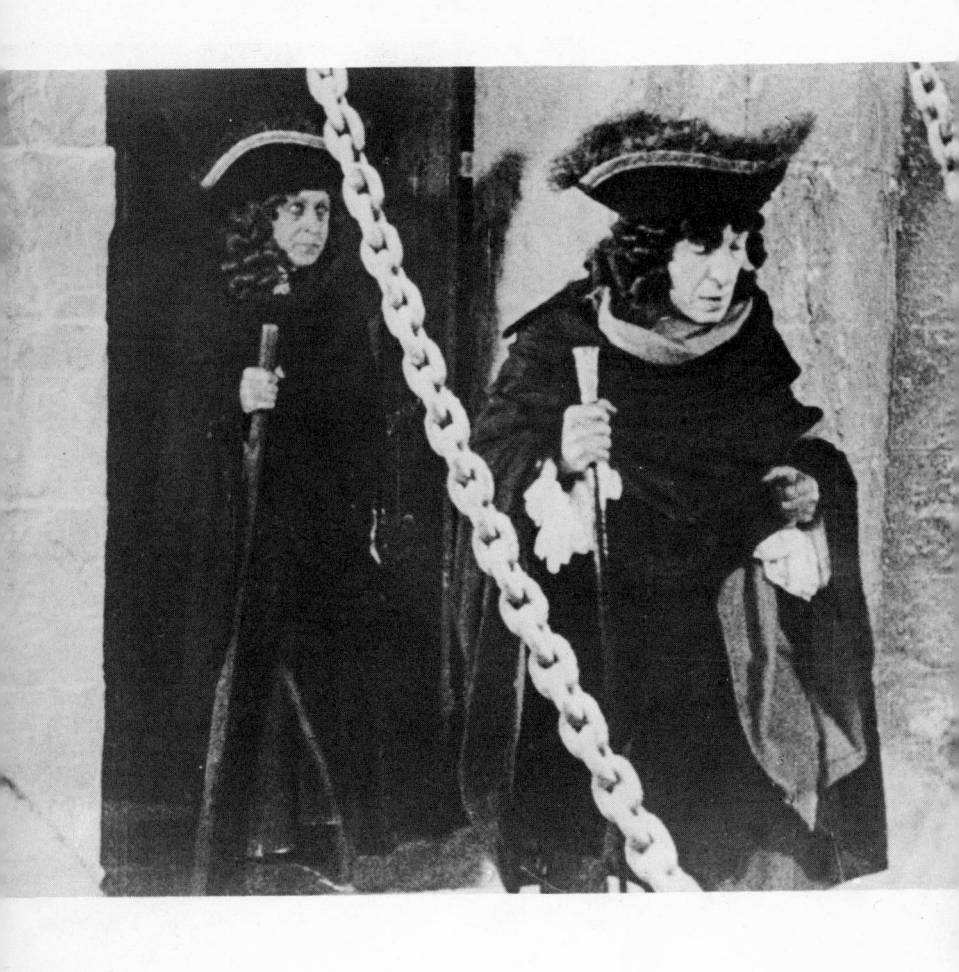

Scenes from *L'Age d'Or*

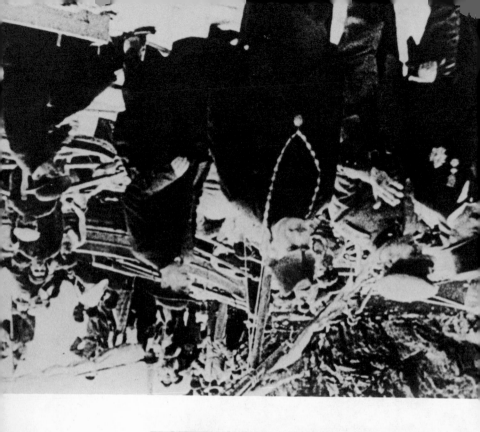
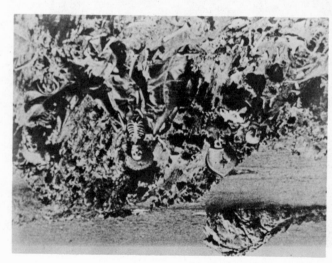

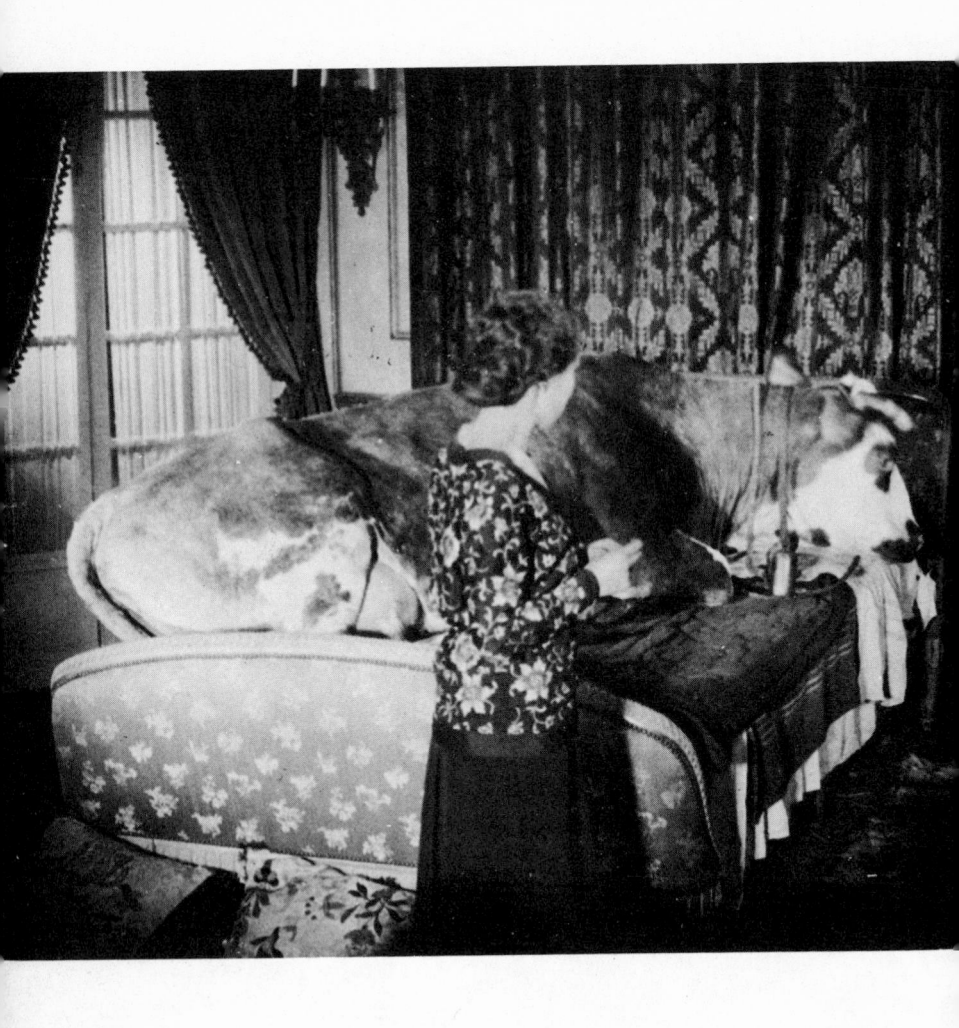

Scenes from *L'Age d'Or*

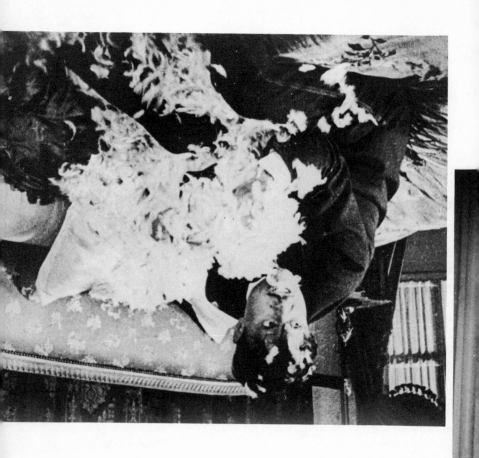

sought to draw some conclusions from the affair and asked themselves: "Is this intervention to be understood as an authorization given equally to those who consider religious propaganda an outrage to break up its manifestations (Roman Catholic propaganda films; pilgrimages to Lourdes and Lisieux; centers of obscurantism like *La Bonne Presse*, meetings of the Index authorities, churches, and so on; perversion of youth in charitable institutions and by military training; sermons over the radio; stores that sell crucifixes and crowns of thorns)?" by using all means at their disposal.

If I have dwelt at length on the scandal that *L'Age d'Or* provoked, it is because its manifold developments contain the most striking arguments for the importance of this work, which is even today the perfect example of the full-length surrealist film. The film was upsetting, hence necessary. Until 1930 the cinema was, with rare exceptions, bland, Therefore, it was not fulfilling its purpose. *L'Age d'Or* had the courage to show the cinema's potential. There was no longer an excuse for making insipid films in which soda pop is passed off as strong drink. It could reveal man to himself. One should always suspect films that provoke an enthusiastic response in those who have no right to like them. Buñuel, upsetting even the cynical hopes some of his enemies might have had for him, perfectly achieved his aim. He created a film that is magnetic in the highest degree for those who *love* and *live,* but murder for the living dead, the dodderers, and those who paddle in the cesspools of reaction.

Buñuel was not in Paris when the scandal over *L'Age d'Or* broke. In fact, he had been invited to Hollywood right after the first private screening.

That first private showing, prologue to the whole incident, was interesting in itself. The producer of the film, the Vicomte de Noailles, was delighted to have a film of his very own (although he knew nothing of the subject, Buñuel always having refused to tell him the details). He invited "all Paris" to the première. A liveried footman at the door called out the guests' names and the de Noailles' received amid smiles, bows, and anticipatory congratulations. It was different after the screening, which had taken place in glacial silence. With eyes averted, the guests fled, and the

de Noailles', crimson with embarrassment, did not know where to hide their heads. As for Buñuel, he had never been happier—at last, the shame he had felt at the admiration of the "bourgeoisie" for *Un Chien Andalou* had been expunged.

So, in 1930, Buñuel made a quick trip to Hollywood, where, morose and aggressive, he watched the making of a Greta Garbo film. One day the M-G-M producer Irving Thalberg asked Buñuel, as a Spaniard, to give his impression of a Spanish-language film starring Lili Damita. Morose and aggressive, as always, Buñuel replied, "I don't care to listen to prostitutes." He was soon dropped by Hollywood and he returned to Spain.

LAS HURDES (Land Without Bread)

While in Spain, Buñuel read a book by Maurice Legendre about Las Hurdes, an impoverished region of that country. Here was a film for him—but where would he find the necessary money? Obviously, no producer would accept such a subject.

He spoke to friends about it. One, an anarchist worker by the name of Ramón Acín, was so carried away by the subject that he told Buñuel, "If I win the lottery, I'll give you my winnings to make your film." He won twenty thousand pesetas. It wasn't a fortune, but it would pay for the trips and the lab work. Yves Allegret paid for the camera rental. Buñuel left for the Hurdes with his associates, Pierre Unik and Éli Lotar.

This time he wanted to make a documentary film. Buñuel understood that reality is sufficiently expressive for one to be able to draw the most profound secrets and mysteries from it without having to underline each flash of insight. He set up his camera in the narrow streets of those villages without chimneys where men live—and, especially, die—the way the officials would have liked the lovers of *L'Age d'Or* to live and die.

This terrifying masterpiece is a kind of testimony. Whenever it is shown, it upsets the digestions of those whose stomachs are too full. The average viewer leaves the film enriched by a healthful

hatred for those who are, in the last analysis, responsible for what it shows. Without shame, equally without ostentation, avoiding any bombast or preachments, Buñuel has filmed the empty belly of the most wretched misery. The idiots, the corpses, the stinking poor of *Las Hurdes* are clearly an extension of the two films that preceded it, the image of a world in which "Imperial Rome" has definitely triumphed. It is also the image of a world in which the protective casing has been ripped off and the inner works exposed, revealing the truth.

Buñuel shot on location for a month, without actors, sets, or script—he was filming a documentary. And yet, this film in no way differs from *L'Age d'Or*. Its realism is the same, and therefore so is its surrealism. Buñuel is as present in this one as in the other.

The peasants of Las Hurdes obviously live as the film shows them to us, but Buñuel has them *act* in the same way as he had Modot act. When the standard rules of cinematic realism are followed films are produced that have no interest because—if we except a few rare cases where chance has intervened to strike off sparks—the day-by-day, even if it is exotic, is a superficial titillation; it is the pleasure a fool feels when he sees himself in a mirror, never imagining that behind the mirror Alice's whole universe lives. Buñuel recreates reality to offer it to us in its entirety, and the documentary lends itself exceptionally well to passing through the mirror. The realistic film makers could have spent years in the dirty streams of Las Hurdes without being able to capture its essence.

The approach is characteristic. The narrator says that goats often fall from the steep rocks and are killed; at that moment we see a puff of smoke* in the lower left corner of the screen, and, from the top of a rock, a goat falls. This shot from a gun—which is not even concealed—sums up the despair of those who for cen-

---

* The print of *Las Hurdes* which is in the film library of the Museum of Modern Art shows neither the gun nor the puff of smoke. When the publishers asked Buñuel whether these details might have been cut from the original, he replied, "Maybe that whole story about the gun and the goat is true. Anyway, I don't think it's at all important." When they discussed this discrepancy with his son, Juan, he claimed that his father had shot the goat himself in order to get this sequence.

turies have seen one of their scarce means of subsistence disappear *without a gunshot*. The puff of smoke was Buñuel's eye that saw (and made us see) beyond the axis of its vision. He takes no sides, because vision itself implies taking a position, and the spectator cannot fail to do the same.

Another example: A donkey carrying some beehives shies and his load falls to the ground, whereupon hundreds of bees attack the animal. Buñuel's group could have rescued the donkey, but they did not (in fact, they may have helped the bees escape from the hives), because the shot of the cruelly stung donkey and the shot of the dog tearing away at the cadaver bring us a step nearer to understanding. In this instance, there is another element at work: Buñuel's violence, of which we will have more to say later.

The extraordinary triple counterpoint on which *Las Hurdes* is built has often been analyzed. The shots in themselves are terrifying: sick people, idiots, corpses, churches, sordid poverty. Their full horror is underscored by the dry, factual style of the commentary, which resembles one that might accompany a documentary on the cultivation of peas in the lower Pyrenees. The commentator remarks in his neutral voice: "There are many cretins," while on the screen we see creatures that not even Zurbarán would have imagined. At this point, insipid romantic music reinforces the image, much as a piece of royal-blue velvet would enhance the horror of a shrunken head placed upon it. Let us not forget that music played the same role in *L'Age d'Or*. (They say that when Buñuel had to choose a piece of music among several of the same kind for this film, he preferred the one he used simply because it was called *Tristan und Isolde*.)

The three elements—image, commentary, and music—add up to an explosive mixture of unique power. Thus the unusual is constantly emphasized, just as the vapid picture hung on the school wall in one of the towns filmed is, thanks to its visual context, shown in all its ignominy.

The dramatic architecture of the film is based on the phrase "Yes, but . . ." That is to say, Buñuel shows an opening scene that is unbearable, then projects a ray of hope, and ends up by destroying that hope. For instance, bread is unknown, *but* from

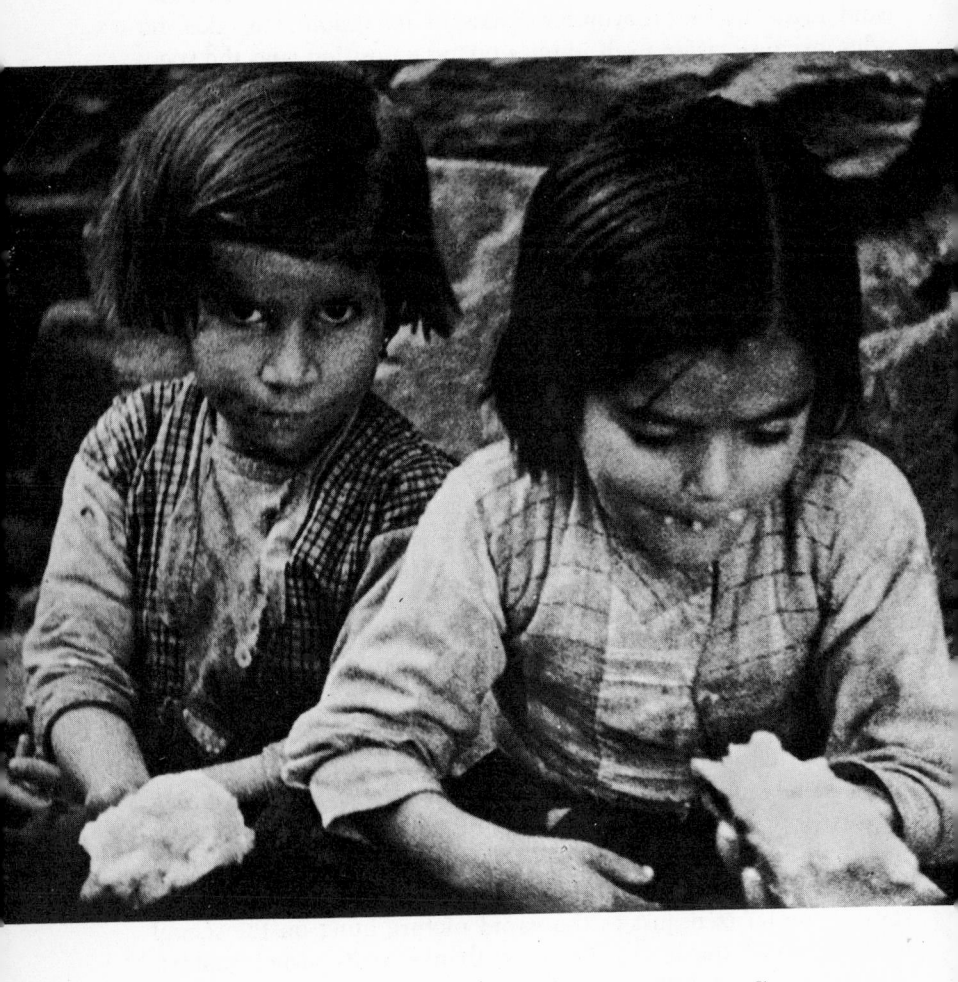

Scene from *Las Hurdes* (Land Without Bread)

time to time the schoolmaster gives a slice to the children, *but* the parents, who fear anything they don't know, throw the bread away. Again, the peasants are often bitten by snakes, *but* the poison is never fatal, *but* the peasants make the bite fatal by trying to cure it with herbs that infect the wound. Each sequence is based on these three propositions, and the progression into horror reaches extremes that can only lead to revolt.

The cold, distant commentary, as has already been pointed out, never takes sides and never draws conclusions. There is no need to do so, for Buñuel, plunging well below surface reality, gives us all aspects of the case.

Thus, for example, the commentator says: "The monks live like hermits, surrounded by a few servants." The word "servant" has no gender, but the camera focuses on a young peasant woman, and the spectator supplies the inference. Another example: "In this wretched land, the only buildings we have seen that give any hint of luxury are the churches." Juxtaposing the hovels in which families and animals live pell-mell in utter filth with the prosperous churches provides more impact than a long speech. It is all as clear as the phrase a ragged, underfed urchin writes on a school blackboard: "Respect the property of others."

A rather curious sequence is introduced into this "documentary." It is a little course of instruction about the anopheles mosquito, illustrated with text-bookish etchings. Here we have a very brief classic documentary, but it is its absolute classicism that makes it one of the more unusual parts of the film, its didactic quality transforming the sequence into an expression of the grotesque. At first sight, this is simply a cultural diversion, but, slit by the razor blade of *Un Chien Andalou*, it assumes the aspect of a nightmare, which fixes on an object of no particular interest with such obsessive clarity that the object is transformed and its magical aspects are revealed. The same thing happens when we study an object in such minute detail that we lose all sense of what it was originally. In this way we reach the unexplorable spheres of reality. The scorpion sequence in *L'Age d'Or* develops in large part from the same state of mind. Similarly, *Las Hurdes* transcends its original meaning. It is no longer a question merely of

the Hurdanos, for, thanks to the magnetic vision of Buñuel, we touch the farthest shores of the super-real. And this above all is why the film is such a tremendous denunciation, for Buñuel is not only criticizing a given state of affairs but pointing out to us the paths of a great, enriching vision.

Despite what some critics have claimed, *Las Hurdes* is just as powerfully surrealist as is *L'Age d'Or*. Buñuel's healthfully corrosive vision could only be surrealist. Without this vision, *Las Hurdes* would be purely documentary. *Las Hurdes* is not art; it is the brutal cry of a man expressing himself freely—the shout of a surrealist.

PEREGRINATIONS

After *Las Hurdes*, Buñuel decided not to direct any more films. For two years he worked at dubbing for Paramount in Paris.

In 1934, he had a serious attack of sciatica. At that point, he wanted to give up film work for good, but nevertheless he agreed to go to Spain to supervise the dubbing of films for Warner Brothers.

In Spain, in 1935, he started to make films again, thanks to his friend Ricardo Urgoito, From 1935 to 1937, he produced four full-length films: *Don Quintín el Amargo,* directed by Luis Machina, a characteristically Madrileño comedy, full of plays on words; *La Hija de Juan Simón,* directed by José Luis Saénz de Heredia, with Carmen Amaya in her first film role; *Quién Me Quiere a Mí?,* a comedy Buñuel has apparently almost entirely forgotten since he can give neither the name of the director nor the subject of the film; *Centinela! Alerta!,* directed by Grémillon, with whom Buñuel had come from France. Grémillon "got bored" during the filming, and Buñuel finished the job. According to him, the film is of no interest whatever.

In addition to these, he produced a short documentary, *Madrid 36,* a part of the series *España Leal en Armor.*

Buñuel can remember nothing more about these productions. He swears that they are best forgotten.

When the Spanish Civil War broke out, the Loyalist government sent Buñuel to Paris on an assignment at the Spanish Embassy. He acted as supervisor on J.-P. Chanois' documentary film, *Espagne 39*. Then, in 1938, he was sent on a diplomatic mission to Hollywood to act as technical adviser on films about the Spanish War.

He started work on *Cargo of Innocence,* but, as Franco was beginning to get the upper hand, M-G-M decided to stop production of pro-Loyalist films, and the project was suspended.

At this juncture, Buñuel's age group was called up, but the defeat of the Republican forces followed so soon thereafter that he had no time to return to Spain to fight.

Without work, without money, Buñuel wandered around Hollywood until Iris Barry, then director of the film library of the Museum of Modern Art, invited him to New York in connection with several anti-Nazi film projects she had in mind. Let me quote directly from notes on a conversation with Buñuel some remarks on the years that followed (1939-47):

"I put together a montage of German documents on the Congress of Nuremberg and the attack on Poland. Out of some twenty-eight reels, I made a film of nine. They showed it to René Clair, who is quoted as saying, 'We're done for!' And they showed it to Chaplin, who laughed uproariously—why, I never knew.

"I worked for Rockefeller on propaganda films aimed at North and South America. They were about 'the great American army,' in English, Spanish, and Portuguese.

"I was dropped from the project because Dali called me an atheist. The directors of the Museum of Modern Art defended me, but I resigned, partly to avoid the publicity and partly because independent production was not possible at the Museum.

"At that time, I was utterly absorbed by the war. I had one aim: Get the Nazis! I became a public speaker.*

"In 1945, at the end of the war, I was in Los Angeles, where I had worked out a film project with Man Ray. The action was to take place in a sand quarry where there was a huge pile of refuse.

---

* When the publishers asked Mr. Buñuel for further details on this phase of his career he replied: "I was not a professional speaker. At one point I was short of money, so I spoke in two or three films for the American army."

"Then I became a 'producer' for Warner Brothers. I drew a salary without having much to do. The firm had plans for making foreign versions of its films, but, as it turned out, I had nothing to do but dubbing. I worked on ten or fifteen films for them.

"I had earned a lot of money, so I could afford a whole year off. I left for Mexico in 1947."

MEXICO

Buñuel went to Mexico because the producer Denise Tual had hired him to do an adaptation of *La Casa de Bernarda Alba,* by Federico García Lorca. But Lorca's family refused to cede the rights and the project was abandoned.

Oscar Dancigers then asked him to direct a musical, *Tampico* —afterward called *Grand Casino.* "It's an idiotic film,"* he says, "but clean, with a few interesting scenes and trick devices. . . . There is a love scene in the mud, really filmed in the mud. There's not a single kiss in the film." It was a box-office failure and Buñuel was once more without work for a period of two years.

In 1949, he directed *El Gran Calavera* (*The Great Madcap*), a comedy with Fernando Soler. It was originally a play, adapted by Luis Alcoriza, from a story by Adolfo Torrado, more or less in the manner of *A Thousand and One Nights,* and it was filmed in two weeks. "It was a clean job but without any scenes of real interest." This was a great box-office success.

This permitted Buñuel to make *Los Olvidados* (*The Young and the Damned*). Here, for the first time since *Las Hurdes,* is an incontestably Buñuelian film. But Buñuel was no longer working independently. He had become involved with that terrifying machine, the commercial cinema. He wanted to prove that he could do commercially successful films without abdicating any part of himself. Is it not rare for a director to work on assigned, insipid,

* I have had to rely on whatever details Buñuel has been willing to give me about the films of his Mexican period that I have not seen. For that reason, I would advise skepticism about his evaluations, because like every overanxious creator, Buñuel is highly critical of his own work.—A.K.

foolish subjects without betraying himself, without having to do something against his own nature and ideas? After so many years, with *Los Olvidados* Buñuel had a passionately interesting subject —a very difficult subject, certainly, but one worthy of him.

It was a great victory for him, because with this film he reached the general public for the first time. It is true that Buñuel has always worked on a broad canvas and addressed himself to the general public rather than to a coterie of specialists, or the "initiate." Now, however, for the first time—and for the simple reason that in *Los Olvidados* Buñuel's unusual elements are presented in a context that does not disturb the public's habits—moviegoers let themselves be carried away by the strange and violent world the film presents.

The film is about the children of large cities, delinquent of necessity, and in self-defense against their families, pederasts, the police. There is no moralizing, as in American films of the same type; rather, the film testifies to the great distress of our times, and its clear vision—so clear as to pierce the husk of daily reality— reveals purely surrealist images: a blind cripple opens his sightless eyes, unable to see that a streetwalker is eying him; a legless man, thrown from his little wheeled platform, flails about on a deserted street like some strange, apocalyptic animal; milk runs down the thighs of a little girl; a cock, angel of misfortune, stridently announces great catastrophes to come; a dove with magic curative powers caresses the naked back of a suffering woman. . . .

With *L'Age d'Or*, Buñuel discovered daily reality in the superreal; with *Los Olvidados* a new series of films begins, each more marvelous than the last, in which the super-real appears beneath the real. It should be noted that if there are dreams and hallucinations in *Los Olvidados* and in nearly all the early Mexican films (*Subida al Cielo, El, Abismos de Pasión, Robinson Crusoe*), since *Ensayo de un Crimen** Buñuel has not needed these subterfuges to transport us to his world.

Of the delightful film *Susana* (the French distributors "en-

---

* Shown in New York City in 1962 under the title, *The Criminal Life of Archibaldo de la Cruz*.

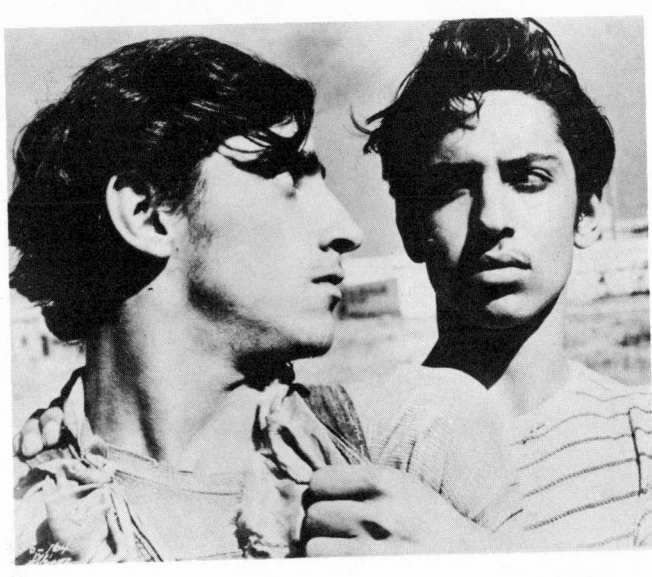

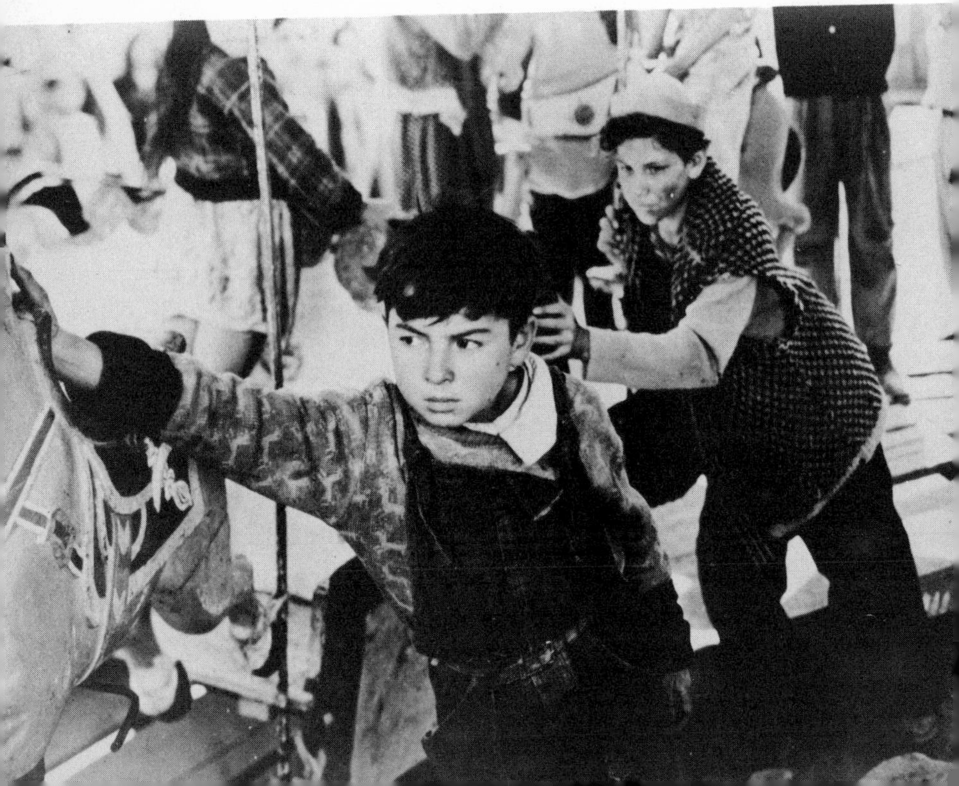

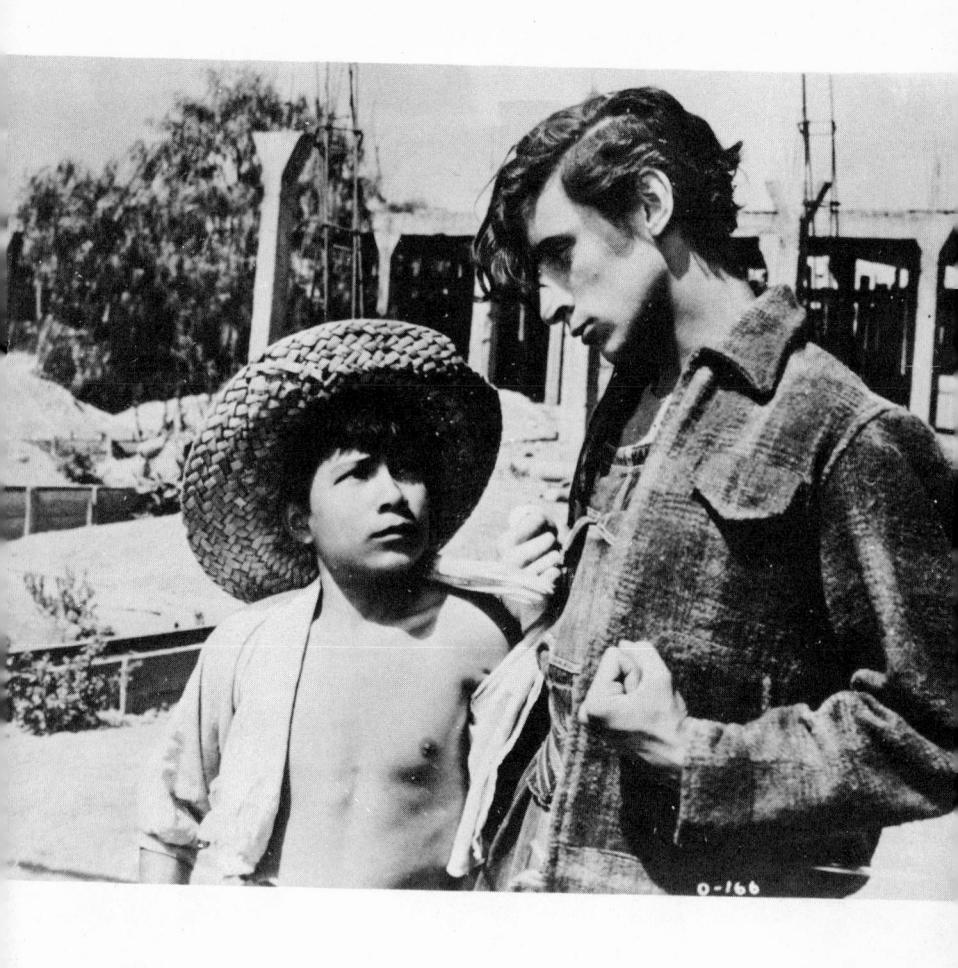

Scenes from *Los Olvidados* (The Young and the Damned)

Scenes from *Los Olvidados* (The Young and the Damned)

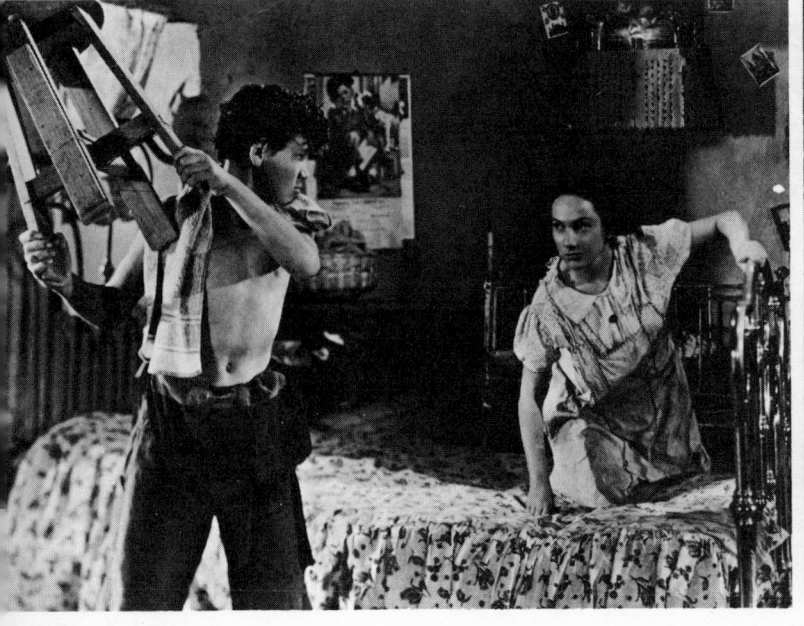
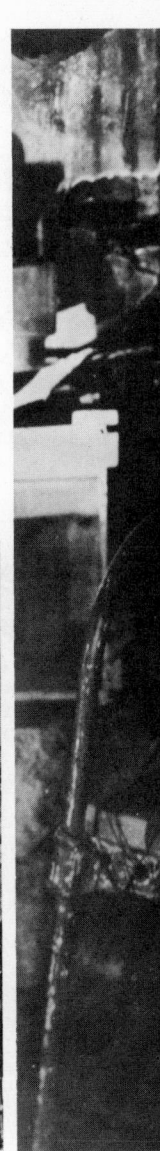

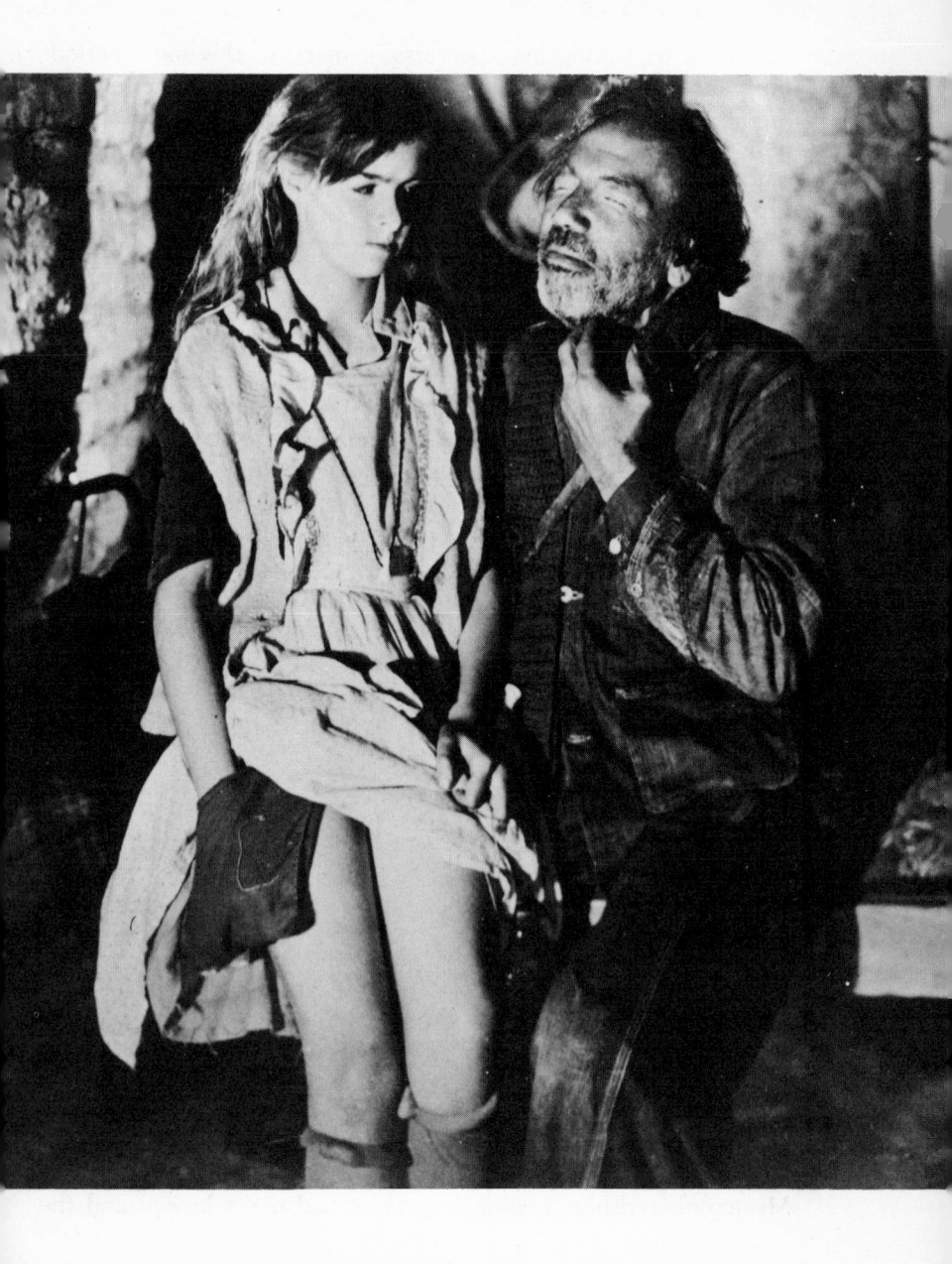

riched" it by calling her "perverse"), made in this same period, Buñuel says "My worst film!" He is certainly right if one looks at the film without knowing its author, who, finding himself saddled with a frightful melodrama replete with every known cliché, attempted to demolish the idiocy by exaggeration. The dialectical bridge from quantity to quality gives, in this instance, some surprising results. An extremely loose young woman spreads consternation throughout the hacienda of an ultra-bourgeois family. The girl is too loose, the bourgeois are too bourgeois, and Buñuel enjoys himself. After all, isn't Susana the most sympathetic character in the film?

If Buñuel now disowns the picture, it is because he had wanted an ending that would have made his humor explicit: Susana would remain at the hacienda, over which she would reign as absolute mistress. Instead, she is punished, but this "moral" ending is treated in so broad a fashion that one must really not know Buñuel at all to take it seriously.

Buñuel's next film, *La Hija del Engaño* (*Daughter of Deceit*), was an "amusing" remake, according to him, of *Don Quintín el Amargo*, which he had produced before the Spanish Civil War.

As to *Una Mujer sin Amor*, we know only that it was an adaptation of de Maupassant's *Pierre et Jean*. Buñuel will not talk about it.

By this time he had become a true Mexican and a recognized director, turning out two or even three films a year.

EXPERIMENTS AND SUCCESSES

After *Los Olvidados*, we witness a slow progression toward an expression freed from commercial contingencies. This development was helped by the Mexican nature of the films Buñuel completed. If he remained Spanish in his violence, and French in his humor, he still needed a favorable atmosphere in which to work. Mexico offered him a calm such as he had never known and the

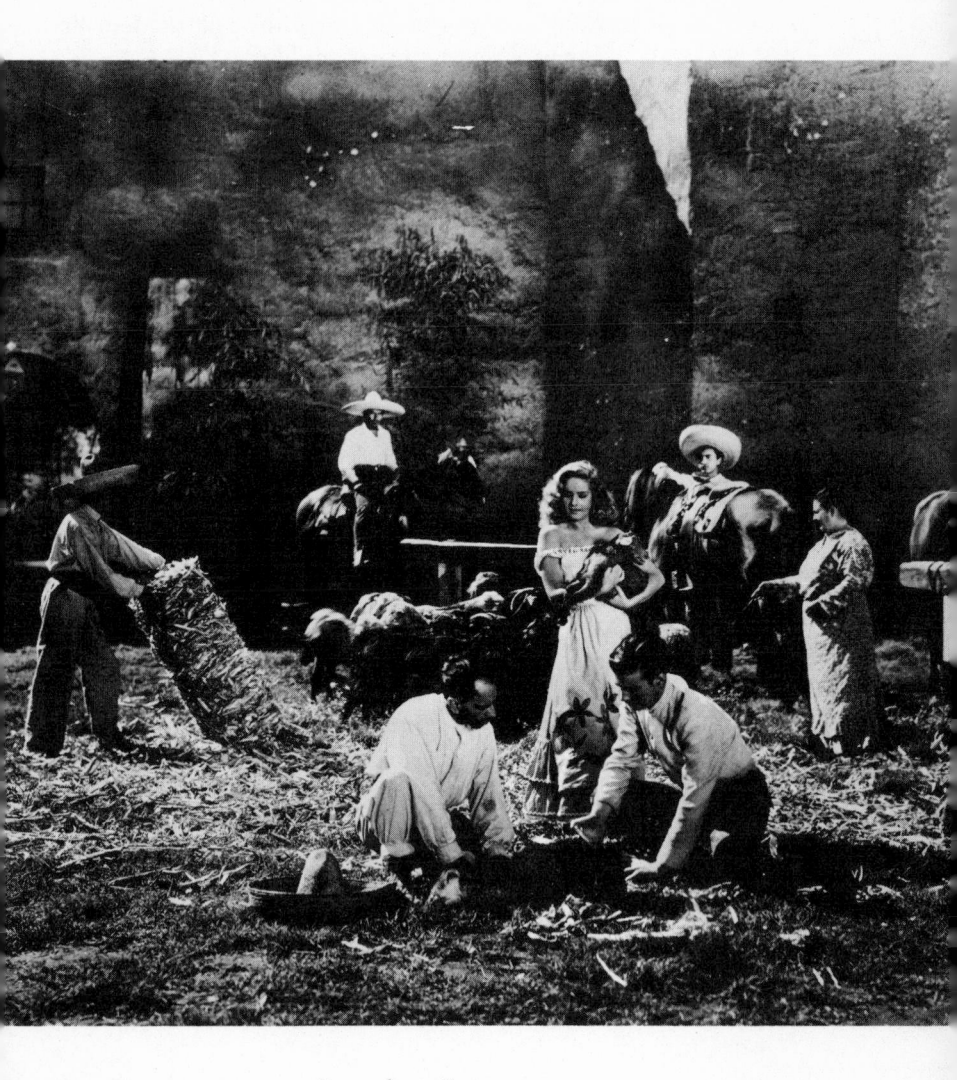

Scene from *Susana*

possibility of working freely without a world of officialdom that was too aware of the explosive nature of his films.

As far as Mexico was concerned, Buñuel was simply a good commercial film director who could turn out a powerful work such as *Los Olvidados,* but who was good above all at harmless comedies and successful melodramas.

This attitude accounts for his *Subida al Cielo* and *El Bruto.*

The first is a relaxed comedy with a hint of something more meaningful just beneath the surface. A young man on a motor trip discovers life and learns to know people and things. It is a modern version of the picaresque tales that Buñuel so loves. The trip begins, in fact, with an absurd birth and ends with a ridiculous death. Meanwhile, the young man has learned what love is, has flirted with politics, had deflated a few balloons: business, the family, folklore, and so on. Delicious details—Buñuel's characteristic humor—abound. Who can forget the one-legged man who can't get his peg leg out of the chamber pot, or the tiny girl who hauls out the submerged auto while playing by the river.

El Bruto is a sublime melodrama. The hired assassin of a rich landowner betrays his boss after he has known love. All the elements of traditional melodrama are there, but they are transfigured by the social implications of the subject and by Buñuel's vision, which always leads to the surrealistic in what is apparently so realistic a film: the grandfather gets up at night to steal chocolates; the slaughterhouses are protected by a picture of the Virgin Mary; the rooster is terrifying; and a love as pure as that in *L'Age d'Or* helps men discover life and their own destinies. Though *El Bruto* is a minor film, it is one of Buñuel's best directed.

After these two trial runs, he gives us a real masterpiece in *El.* This film has been the subject of much discussion. Certainly it is far more than a clinical study of jealousy. It is a return to the theme of *L'Age d'Or,* and the first link in the chain binding *L'Age d'Or* to *Viridiana.*

Buñuel's evolution is unique in the history of the cinema. His first three films—*Un Chien Andalou, L'Age d'Or* and *Las Hurdes*—seemed freely to reflect his interior world. Then, and for too long an intermission, he was obliged to turn to commercial work. With

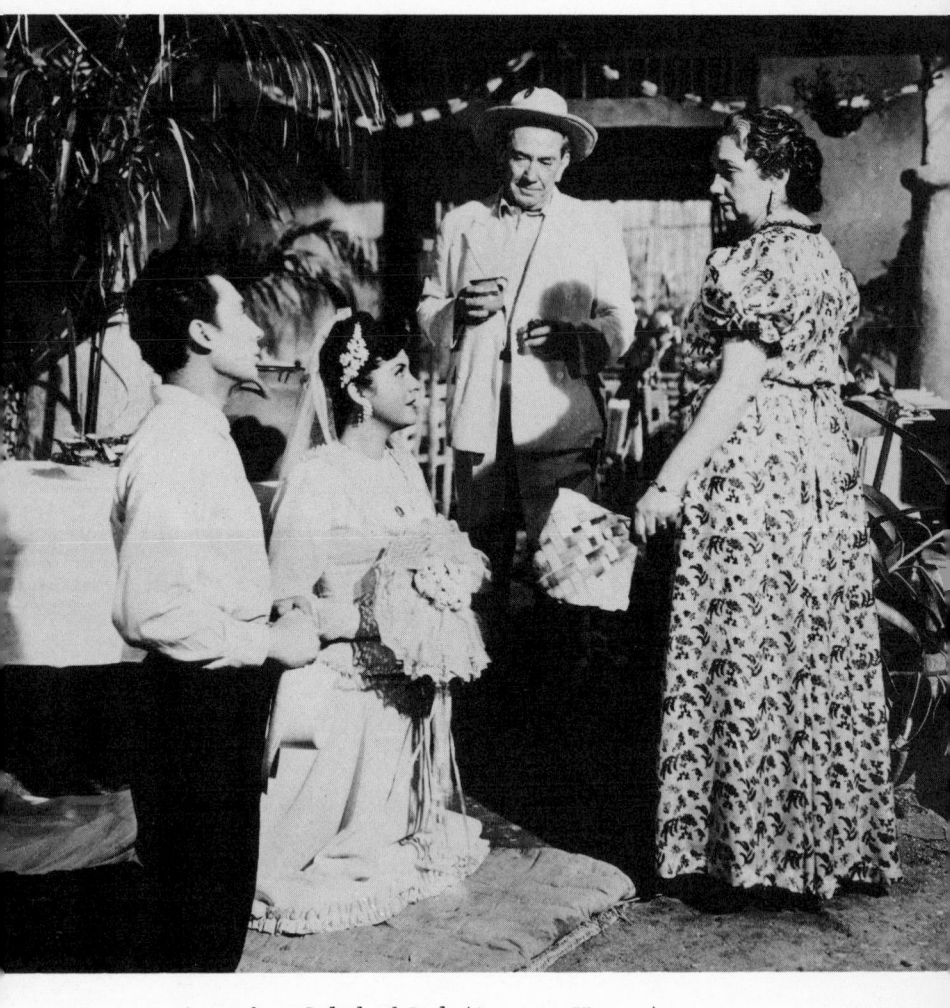

Scene from *Subida al Cielo* (Ascent to Heaven)

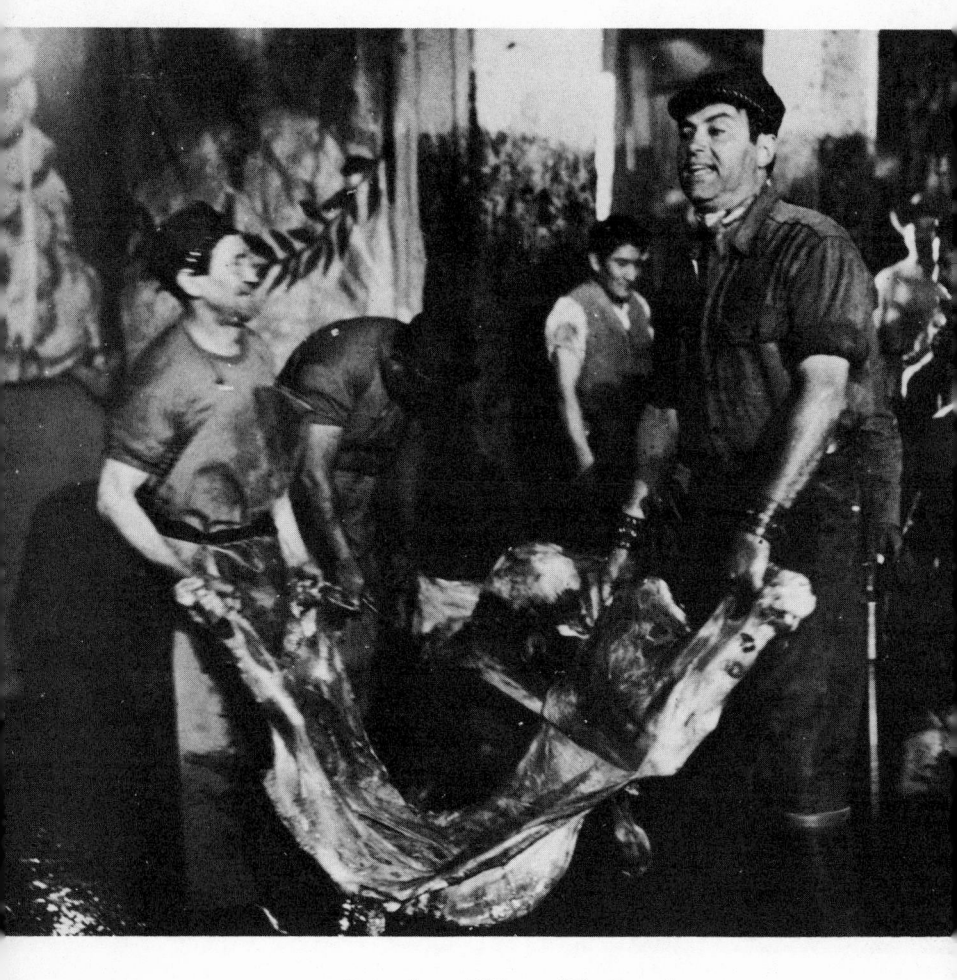

Scene from *El Bruto* (The Brute)

the best will in the world, he could not prevent certain elements of his "self" from penetrating the commercial films—instinctive, subconscious, hence surrealistic, elements. Little by little, these elements took more and more space, sometimes destroying the commercial canvas.

It was this process that led us to *Viridiana*, but the long dalliance in the dangerous waters of commercialism gave us back a more mature Buñuel, mentally even freer than in *L'Age d'Or*, a Buñuel purer than the man who made *Un Chien Andalou*, more vitriolic than the man who made *Las Hurdes*.

But let us not get ahead of ourselves. *El* marked an important date; it took up once more the subject of *L'Age d'Or*. The influence of de Sade is everywhere apparent in a scenario that the majority of the Mexican public took for a run-of-the-mill melodrama on jealousy.

The hero of *El*, Francisco, is another Modot, as we saw him in the love-torture scene and the solitude sequence in *L'Age d'Or*. He is a man looking for absolute love; he wants to be a free man, but, though he is over forty, he is still a virgin, so great is his attachment to the moral rules of our saintly society. Bourgeois to the depths of his tranquil soul, he is a perfect example of the right-thinking cretin created out of whole cloth by the church, family, army, schools, and all the other institutions that aim at destroying human freedom.

This perfect man finally finds absolute love, and it comes as a rude shock to all his aspirations and habits. But it is too late; he cannot live his love; and when he comes to understand that his only solution is to kill all bourgeois morality—personified by the priest—he is shut up in the most cruel of prisons, the monastery. The woman he loves is a personification of de Sade's *Justine*. *El* is a new version of the last two sequences of *L'Age d'Or*.

L'Age d'Or was also the point of departure for one of Buñuel's most misunderstood but most important films, *Abismos de Pasión*. The abysses of passion conceal an absolutely personal interpretation of the last part of Emily Brontë's *Wuthering Heights*, on which William Wyler had already based a mediocre film.

Once again, the subject is an absolute love, and again, as in

Buñuel (extreme left) on location in Mexico during the filming of *El* (He)

Arturo de Cordova in *El*

L'Age d'Or, all the love scenes of the film are underlined by the music of *Tristan und Isolde.*

Ever since the filming of *L'Age d'Or* Buñuel had worked on an adaptation of *Wuthering Heights.* His Mexican film almost always follows the shooting script he had done in Paris, which is why he calls this film "outdated." Yet he admits that the last sequence, which takes place in the tomb, is interesting. It is, in fact, sublime: the imaginary world, passion, total love that dares face down death—all these themes so dear to Buñuel come together in five minutes that are among the most overwhelming, visually as well as emotionally, that the human spirit has given us.

A PERIOD OF CALM

All Buñuel's Mexican films up to and including *Abismos de Pasión* testify to an anxiety caused in large measure by the unconfessed conflict in a man who proclaimed far and wide how much he detested the cinema but who could not keep from making films. Buñuel's frustration was abysmal. He cared nothing about the business aspects of films, but he was unwilling or unable to see to what extent his own films—according to him, highly commercial —were notably noncommercial.

A new attitude toward his work became perceptible in certain films of this period. He accepted what he was doing; he began to understand that he would have no difficulty in ridding himself of his few remaining shackles. To do so he needed, perhaps, to work with a novel that is as famous as it is dreadful. He chose *Robinson Crusoe.* The fact that he could masterfully overcome such a major limitation gave him a quiet self-confidence that grew more and more pronounced in the period leading up to *Viridiana.* He no longer detested films—*his* films.

Defoe's middle-class hero, who can think of no use for his new freedom other than to recreate on his island all the elements of his past life, becomes in Buñuel's hands a genuinely tragic personality, lost amid his own contradictions. Like Brecht, although

Dan O'Herlihy as Robinson Crusoe and James Fernandez as Friday in *Robinson Crusoe*

without Brecht's drive to prove a point, Buñuel makes use of a supremely unsympathetic hero to pass judgment on two flaws. One: Robinson Crusoe is a Christian. However, in critical moments, either the Bible makes no sense or its meaning becomes completely atheistic. When he is teaching Friday Christian theology, the young Negro has the healthy reactions of the dying man replying to the priest (see de Sade and also the plague sequence in *Nazarín*): "So your God wanted to do everything the wrong way just to tempt his creature? To test him? He didn't know him for what he was, then? He didn't fear the outcome?"

Two: Robinson is a colonialist. His first reaction upon finding Friday is to chain him. Furthermore, he wants to make "a civilized man" of him. But a man of Friday's moral health cannot be enslaved, and Robinson is conquered by Friday, who teaches him respect, friendship, and human solidarity.

A third major theme transfigures the film. This is the exceedingly complex problem of solitude—with all its involvements, such as fears, hallucinations, masturbation, etc.—that so obsesses Buñuel.

And, finally, there is the element of eroticism. Buñuel managed to make an erotic work out of a book that has not one woman in it. No one will readily forget the extraordinary scene in which Robinson, using a woman's dress to fashion a scarecrow, watches as a light breeze rises and makes the dress come alive, become a woman.

With *Robinson Crusoe*, Buñuel attempted color for the first time, which gives the film a Rousseau-like accent appropriate to the profound relationship that exists between Buñuel and things, that is, between him and the natural, material world. This rapport, apparent for the first time in *Robinson Crusoe*, is associated with the recently discovered calm I mentioned above.

His next film, *La Ilusión Viaja en Tranvía* (*Illusion Travels by Streetcar*), is a minor but charming work that tells, in the picturesque tone Buñuel manages so well, of the crazy night ride of a trolley car. Two sequences are worthy of inclusion in a Buñuel anthology: the theatrical performance of a Biblical subject, and the sequence in which the slaughterhouse butchers use

the trolley's baggage racks as butcher hooks. Also to be noted are the two little old ladies who carry around the statue of a saint, with whose help they live handsomely off that form of Christian blackmail called charity.

I am not familiar with *El Río y la Muerte*, apparently an intensely interesting film—and incomprehensible anywhere but in Mexico, it seems—which deals with the fascination of death and the facility with which some Mexicans kill each other over nothing. "There are seven deaths, four burials, and I don't know how many wakes in the film," Buñuel once observed.

The last film in his first Mexican period is the delicious, adorable, sublime *Ensayo de un Crimen*—a farce, but, as in all Buñuel's farces, we grit our teeth as we laugh. Archibaldo, the son of a middle-class family, dresses up in his mother's corsets and undergarments; while still a boy he persuades himself that a music box he owns has the power to kill anyone who gets in his way. All his life long he tries to kill someone, but by misadventure all his intended victims are snatched from him. Either they die accidentally or they are killed by someone else. Poor Archibaldo is betrayed and balked at every turn. His frustrated drive becomes more and more obsessional for, like his near relative in *El*, Francisco, he is Christian and helpless. He is quite serious when he says to the nun he is aiming to murder: "You love God, Sister?"

"Of course."

"Your dearest wish, Sister, is to be near Him as soon as possible, is it not?"

"Of course."

"Then, Sister, rejoice!" And he takes out his razor to despatch the good woman to heaven, which she reaches on her own by dint of falling down an elevator shaft.

Later, he plans to kill his wife as she is reciting her prayers, the fatal blow to be delivered as she is saying "Amen."

The most disturbing sequence in this refreshing film is with the mannequin. Archibaldo finds a wax mannequin in a dress shop. He manages to trace the human model who posed for the mannequin and can dream of nothing but the murder of this beautiful woman whom he wants to kill by burning, "like Joan of Arc."

Scene from *Ensavo de un Crimen* (The Life of Crime
of Archibaldo de la Cruz) with Ernesto Alonso as
Archibaldo

Accordingly, he invites her to his house, after firing his oven (he is a ceramist), assuring her that she will not be alone. And, indeed, the mannequin, which he has meanwhile bought, is also there. Archibaldo, rebuffed by the living woman, kisses the lips and caresses the breasts of the mannequin, which he has draped in the living model's underwear. Everything is ready for the big holocaust scene when, at the last instant, he is momentarily diverted; the woman escapes, and our magnificent, pitiful hero is left with the mannequin, which he finally burns with as much love as if it were a woman of flesh and blood.

The spectator's uneasiness reaches a peak during this sequence, for Buñuel, following his hero's imagination, substitutes the real woman for the mannequin. We know that the woman has actually left, but we *feel* that these legs Archibaldo is caressing are real legs, that the body he thrusts into the fire is a real body.

The Buñuelian, totally surrealist delirium of this film debouches into a calm close. In *El*, Francisco ends his life in a monastery, simulating serenity. Archibaldo, on the other hand, gets well, conquers his compulsions, and ends his life as a normal man who has thrown away his infernal machine, who shaves with an electric razor, and makes love normally with a wife whom he loves.

Like almost every other Buñuel film, *Ensayo* disintegrates into small bits, sketches, which give it a choppy quality that the conscientious critics would call "poor construction," quite forgetting that Buñuel's films are dreamed rather than organized and that they therefore possess the mysterious associations and the magico-logical continuity of dreams. They are real dreams that draw their virulent strength from daily reality; they are the shrieks of darkest depression that follow the pathways of free association. They are, accordingly, as fragmentary, as incoherent—and just as well constructed—as a dream.

FRENCH FILMS

Buñuel returned to France in 1956. Much water had flowed under the bridges of the Seine since *Las Hurdes*. The man who had once

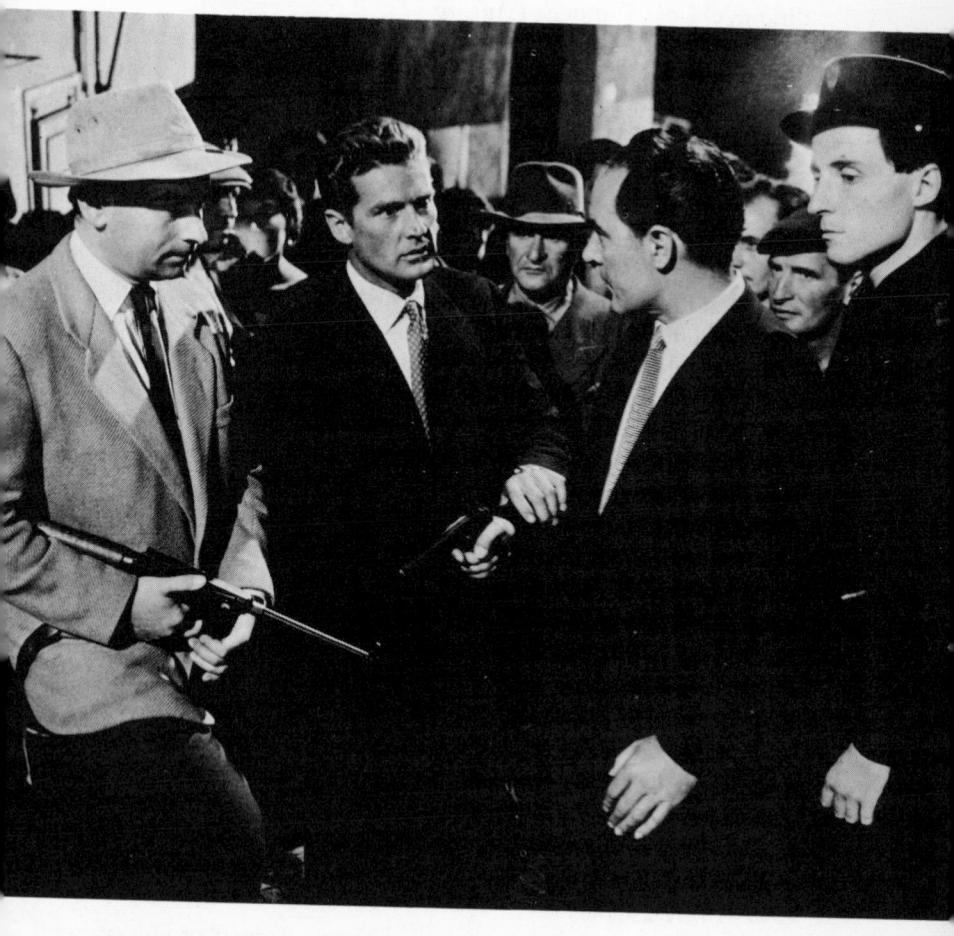

Scene from *Celà s'Appelle l'Aurore* (That Is Called
Dawn)

been thought so dangerous was now deluged with proposals from French producers. Buñuel agreed to film Emmanuel Roblès' splendid novel *Cela S'Appelle l'Aurore*.

His return to France marked both a step forward and a step backward. He advanced in clarity; his social and moral ideas were now precisely defined, and he could call a cat a cat and a cop a cop. Simply, but without simplifying, he produced a truly revolutionary film, a film that dealt with the human condition, solidarity and freedom, the social struggle, indissolubly linked to love.

The regression was more complex. Watching this film, which moves me to the point of tears, I always have the feeling that Luis wanted to prove to the French that they were mistaken in labeling him as raving and incoherent. He kept his virulence but lost his violence. The calm encountered in his last Mexican films here became a "logical" calm. Was it a return to traditional logic? Certainly, the characteristic Buñuelian sequences are not absent —the image of Christ with the electric wires, an unusual tortoise, the cop who reads Claudel and embellishes his desk with Dali's Christ—but the novelty of *L'Age d'Or, El,* and *Ensayo de un Crimen* lay in his way of presenting a violent story with a surrealist point of view. Here the subject is surrealist (revolt and mad love), but the film is not. A dozen directors could have succeeded with *Cela S'Appelle l'Aurore* as well as Buñuel; no one could have done the same with—to give only two examples—*Ensayo* or *Susana*.

In sum, this magnificent film is not characteristic of Buñuel's best surrealist style. It is wholesome only because of its nonconformist subject.

The second French film of this period (1956) was a co-production with Mexico—*La Mort en Ce Jardin,* based on the novel by José-André Lacour.

The scenario was revised several times—French producers tend to meddle in a heavy-handed way—and the film as we know it has only the remotest connection with Buñuel's initial idea. Even so, it is exciting, and can be considered a first draft of *Nazarín.*

The first part is a minute description of a police and military dictatorship, of hopeless revolt, and of the Fascist repression that

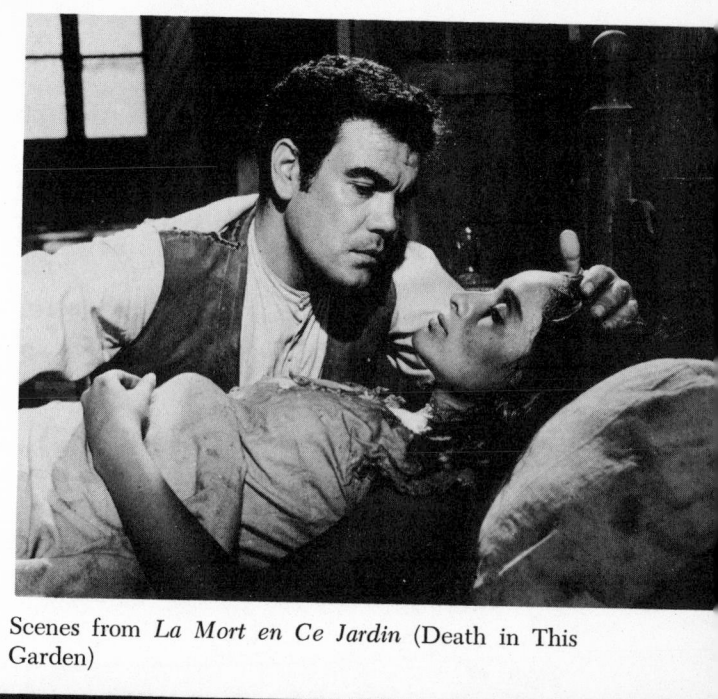

Scenes from *La Mort en Ce Jardin* (Death in This Garden)

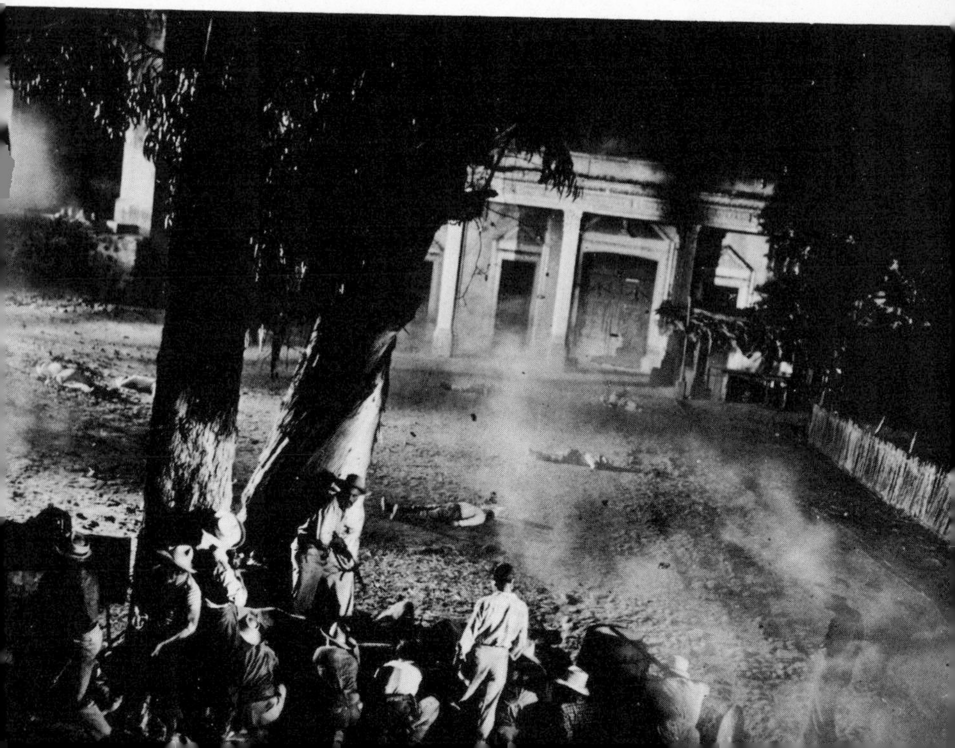

follows. Working in this social context, Buñuel naturally remembered real incidents from the Spanish Civil War. His characters include middle-class Christians, prostitutes, a virile adventurer, a deaf mute (she represents Luis' *fleur bleue* side), and, most important, a priest, Father Lizardi—masterfully portrayed by Michel Piccoli—who is a totally new kind of hero in the history of the cinema.

These magnificent and miserable people are hunted down by the military. Danger frees them all from the tawdry banalities of serene and civilized life, and they discover a mutual solidarity. But to return to the personality of Lizardi: he is likable, he believes sincerely in his "mission," but the poor fellow is an utter fool. He is quite unaware that he is playing handyman to the oppressors; he wears a fine wristwatch, the gift of a foreign colonial firm called Northern Refineries (an obvious allusion to pre-liberation Cuba); he repeats Christ's words that aim to persuade the oppressed to be resigned to their fate—"All they that take the sword shall perish with the sword"; above all, he wants to do good, to reconcile irreconcilables, to re-establish peace by means of the soft answer. He is forever saying "I take it upon myself . . ." as he precipitates some disaster. He believes that he is very strong because he is in possession of "the truth," but he is simply one more victim of reaction in all its forms. Little by little he is obliged to admit the obvious: it is impossible to live as a pure, innocent Christian. The priest becomes a man. Unfortunately, the transformation is of short duration; once the danger has passed, Lizardi becomes again the fumbling simpleton priest, as criminal in his unawareness as ever. He is killed by a religious fanatic, dying at the hands of one of the creatures he himself helped to fabricate.

The film ends on an optimistic note: the positively oriented hero and the deaf mute, who are the sole survivors, leave the murderous jungle and set out for the open sea.

La Mort en Ce Jardin is not a perfect film—far from it. The post-synchronization is notably bad. Yet it commands our sympathetic interest because of its revolutionary spirit and the way in which it shows how impossible it is to be a Christian and at the same

Buñuel with Gerard Philippe (seated at extreme right) in Mexico during the filming of *La Fièvre Monte à El Pao* (The Fever Reaches El Pao)

time to remain pure in spirit and not become a malefic puppet in the hands of those who want to keep the people imprisoned in obscurantism.

Buñuel's third film of this period was *La Fièvre Monte à El Pao*, in which Gérard Philippe appeared for the last time before his death. This could have been a very great work, but unhappily there was so much discussion with the producers, and Buñuel had to alter the scenario so often, that one feels one is seeing merely the outline or rough draft of a potential masterpiece.

The theme is one of burning relevance today, for it concerns the old problem—does the end justify the means? In a country where a dictatorship has been established, an honest young man wants to remain decent; he wants to humanize the regime and its assassins without shedding blood but somehow to accomplish this from "within." This reformer is a kind of lay saint, so artless as to believe that democracy can overthrow Fascism without any clash or violence. He does not realize that his idiotic idealism is the dictatorship's strongest guarantee; far from being afraid of this nonviolent visionary, his masters exploit him, because from time to time they must appear to be liberal toward those who are *not* their enemies.

At the last moment this pitiable hero becomes aware of his complicity and betrayal and pays for this awakening with his life, but his sacrifice excuses nothing; in no way does it redeem him. As one of the characters says, "One second of courage is not enough to redeem years of cowardice."

In my opinion, Buñuel should freely remake this film, for its subject is one of the most profoundly revolutionary ever to be conceived. Even this version is important to one's knowledge of Buñuel's work.

PRIEST AND RACIST

These three attempts at French production—or, rather, co-production—threw a searching light on Buñuel's salutary ideas about

Buñuel (extreme left) directing a scene in *Nazarín*

Scene from *Nazarín*

current social problems, but they in no way advanced the abolishment of rational logic that he had undertaken in some of his Mexican films. He now returned to his new country to make one of the most complex films of his career—*Nazarín*.

This film was much discussed, and a great deal of foolishness has been written about it, while the perennial gravediggers hastened to bury Buñuel under altogether gratuitous praise. Even honest and liberal-minded people were influenced by the press campaign to believe that Buñuel was mellowing, turning into a circumspect moderate—that he was betraying his true nature.

We were told that in his heart of hearts Buñuel was a Christian, that his blasphemies were merely the reflection of a profound faith.

It had never occurred to Buñuel that the acolytes of the established order would find this way to finish him off. Yet for them the order of the day was: "Let us interpret everything that does not suit us in such a way as to destroy it. What we cannot openly fight let us absorb and adopt." Never did this tactic reap so rich a harvest. In the purity of his spirit, Buñuel believes that everyone thinks as he does, that there is no need for him to explain, to strike out against vicious obscurantists.

Nazarín, nonetheless, is a more illuminating character for being simple and direct. He has faith, he believes, he accepts literally what the holy books tell him; he pushes his own desire to be a saintly man to the limit. For this he is attacked from all sides, and he ends by losing his faith. He becomes a man when he discovers that to practice religion entails only misfortune, that it aggravates suffering—when, in a word, he discovers that one can and should substitute solidarity for charity.

The film has been sufficiently dissected (*Viridiana* casts a brilliant light on it) for there to be no further need to explain the evidence showing us that Buñuel is no longer anticlerical—he is an atheist. He is fully self-possessed; his revolt henceforth will be against the basics, he will mine the very foundations and not merely the secondary aspects of that most holy and bourgeois society that oppresses humankind.

The beauty of the photography in *Nazarín* must be emphasized.

Bernie Hamilton and Kay Meersman in *La Jeune Fille*
(The Young One)

A Zurbarán or a Goya could have signed his name to this film. Here, at last, we find ourselves on the elusive dividing line where ideas of the beautiful and the ugly recede to give way to a new idea of what one might call the necessary.

Nazarín is a dazzling explosion in which form and substance, thought and action, are fused in the multitongued fires of the necessary.

Let barking dogs bark. Buñuel is moving forward.

Between *Nazarín* and *Viridiana* he made *La Jeune Fille,* a minor, charming work.

Racism and—if I may coin a word—Lolitism are its subjects. The relationship between the racist and the Negro who is being hunted for rape is somewhat reminiscent of the connection between Robinson and Friday, and the relationship between the racist and the fourteen-year-old girl is the catalyst that, in an unexpected way, will complete the racist's debatable evolution. To be specific: a forty-odd-year-old racist falls in love with a young girl. Society can only condemn this love, as it also condemns the blacks. Suddenly the racist finds himself put on a level with the Negro; he is, however, as innocent as is the Negro, and is obliged to join forces with him (again the theme of solidarity), for the moral fugitive needs the social fugitive and vice versa, social and moral ideas being insolubly connected. Is the racist sincere? Has he come to a real understanding, or is he pretending? Buñuel does not answer the question and leaves each spectator free to answer it according to his own lights.

In this film, where we find several familiar themes, the figures of Lizardi and Nazarín are reflected in the person of the pastor. This pastor is not a racist, yet he insists that the mattress on which he is to sleep be turned because a "nigger" has just slept on it.

In connection with *La Jeune Fille,* I must again point out with what perfect composure Buñuel now approaches all problems: he makes the love of a middle-aged man for a nymphet not only plausible but even moving, so complex and blinding is the face of love.

Then came *Viridiana.*

VIRIDIANA

You may remember Theda Bara and the fact that her name was an anagram of "Arab death." The famous man-eater—or her press agent—had cast about for a lurid label and found one.

With Buñuel it is a very different matter; his choice of the title is, rather, one more triumph of instinct. The essence of the film is condensed in this admirable combination of "virus" and "Diana."

Let us indulge in a little wild speculation. (Isn't Buñuel himself, no matter what he is doing, always in something of a delirium?) The woman who could have been the huntress is attacked by a virus that makes her the quarry instead. The virus is Buñuel; the fabulous woman, who is prepared to explode anything and everything in her path, is that perennial victim of many faces who, from film to film, from *Susana* to *El*, attracts the virus by her femininity—and also by her strength, for victims are often stronger than their tormentors.

The title is happily chosen, then. It is a woman's name, and a woman who bears such a name already exists: she is beautiful, intense, and passionate, but these qualities are smothered by forces as powerful as they are futile. Such is the intelligence of a society that is able to channel mighty currents into seas that are calm and sometimes, in their stagnation, harmful.

As to theme, is there one? Do any of Buñuel's films have a theme? In any event, there is no conventional plot—which is one more way in which Buñuel is a poet.

Nevertheless, the public, snob or not, that frequents the movie houses requires some semblance of a story; *Viridiana*'s is as simple as it is scandalous—scandalous not because it strives to be so, but because it is simple and obvious. At the age of sixty-one, Buñuel had achieved great serenity and lost the desire to shock; he had become a splendid wild creature spreading a salutary fear.

Viridiana is a film that frightens those who have reason to be afraid.

L'Age d'Or was deliberately scandalous. The *Viridiana* scandal is unintentional and intrinsic. Buñuel himself is an object of scandal. He reveals himself in this film, pours all the wealth of his being into it until it bursts into flames. The fire is brilliant, but it is not for everyone.

Viridiana came about in this way. A Mexican producer, commissioning a film, said to Buñuel, "Do whatever you like. I won't interfere." Strangely, incredibly, the producer kept his word. Buñuel wrote his scenario, which he did not even show to the producer, and was preparing to film it in Mexico; the other man, meanwhile, was making financial arrangements for it to be produced in Spain. A co-producer was readily found. Franco and his secret police could hardly keep from tooting a triumphant horn. Think of it! The uncompromising Buñuel, a man who never concealed his—shall we say, unfriendly?—feelings for all dictatorships, but especially for the one that was ravaging his native country, was relenting, returning to the fold. Mere pecadilloes, those youthful excesses; once their rebellious stage is behind them, are not all Spaniards the natural sons of Franco and of that Most Holy and Apostolic Roman Catholic Church? Miró, Picasso, Casals, Buñuel—and why boggle?—even those who died from the bullets of Fascism belong to us—even Lorca. Such is the boundless magnanimity of dictatorships and religion! All the while, the jails are jammed, and poverty lays waste to a magnificent country. In order to survive, men are obliged to become policemen, priests, or pederasts. This is no exaggeration, nor am I straying from my subject. (Do we ever stray from the subject, whatever it may be, if we shout aloud our hatred of dictatorship?)

For years, following a very astute policy, the Franco regime had been trying to recapture Buñuel. In fact, in 1951, when he was in Cannes in connection with the showing of *Los Olvidados,* he had already been officially approached. Fascism knows that it paralyzes all creative expression, and that first it must accept its enemies the better to muzzle them, then appropriate them, and by tarnishing their prestige, destroy them.

To talk to a Spaniard about his homeland is tantamount to winning him over, and Buñuel, who genuinely worships his family, and his mother in particular, had dreamed since 1936 of returning to Spain. And return he did, almost clandestinely, avoiding all publicity. When the producer informed him that *Viridiana* would be filmed in Spain, he agreed. To be once more among friends and brothers, to see and to smell the Spanish earth was, for a man fashioned of longings and dreams and instincts, a rare joy.

He definitely did not want his film to be sugar-coated, however —nor did he *want* to create a scandal. The Spanish censor read the material and found only a few details to be altered. (All censorship offices are staffed on principle with oblivious drones.) The dissatisfaction centered on the film's ending. Buñuel changed it, and in the process transformed it from the mediocre to the sublime. (Presently we will compare the two endings.) So even censorship helped Buñuel. And the bomb burst.

Viridiana is the freest of Buñuel's films that followed *l'Age d'Or*. What I have always loved above all else in him is the naïveté, even the unawareness, with which he injects his personal world into all that he does. Nothing is held back. He is unafraid; he pours forth his image with no qualms about the *déjà vu* or so-called bad taste. *Viridiana* is a film composed (as are *L'Age d'Or* and, to a lesser extent, *El* and *Ensayo de un Crimen*) uniquely of Buñuel's obsessions and manias. *Viridiana* is the second pillar—the other being *L'Age d'Or*—that supports the admirable Buñuelian edifice.

At one extreme, the shock of *L'Age d'Or*, a deliberate blow struck against prohibitions of any kind; at the other, *Viridiana*, created in perfect serenity and perhaps for that reason even more shocking. Buñuel's evolution lies between these poles. As he said to me, "Once upon a time, when I was offered the consecrated wafer I would spit on it; now I simply say, 'I couldn't care less.'" Once upon a time, anticlericalism and blasphemy; today, atheism, total tenderness, lightninglike sympathy for men and things. I have not reached Buñuel's age, but I think that the second attitude—which, for that matter, does not contravene the first but simply goes beyond it—is the more revolutionary. This would be

true, obviously, only in the case of a personality like Buñuel's, containing within it all the forces of moral and social health, which he is able to project on the screen with the complete unself-consciousness of the truly great.

In *Viridiana* Buñuel is no longer trying to convince the public of anything at all; he is no longer interested in generalizations; he simply offers images, his own photographic images, and thereby comes full circle, joining *Viridiana* to *Un Chien Andalou.* But if the earlier film remains pure visual shock, *Viridiana* goes further; it is a supremely profound moral and perceptual shock, for the simple images of Buñuel are at once tender and abusive, grand and strident, sublime and gross—they are like the draperies that hang in romantic rooms where anything can happen.

For all that he is no longer trying to make a point with his public, Buñuel, despite himself, launches into a vast dialogue with those who are prepared to be enriched by the nature of the man who is addressing them.

He used to say to me that it is not his intention to photograph the "impious," and that if there were a "pious" image that seemed to him interesting or sympathetic, he would certainly put it in a film. "But," he added, with a little smile, "no pious images come to mind." There is not a trace of affectation or trickery, much less any calculation, in Buñuel. His eyes are filled with extraordinary images, and we must be grateful to him for showing them to us, for they are the supreme expression of man's total liberation. Buñuel is a free man and believes that others should be as free as he—which is why he sometimes balks at explaining himself. *Viridiana*, however, is so personal a film that no further statement from him is necessary.

Viridiana is a novice in a convent. She is about to take her vows. Her only relative is a somewhat elderly uncle, Don Jaime, of whom she is not very fond because he has never concerned himself with her. Her Mother Superior insists, however, that she go to see her uncle, who has sent for her, before she takes the veil. Viridiana is most reluctant to make the trip. This beautiful young woman is absorbed in her devotion to her God and her convent,

and she has a presentiment that "outside" everything is dangerous; like all people in the grip of false ideals, she fears experiences that threaten to unseal her eyes.

Already in this first sequence we have several Buñuelian themes. Wishing to be "kind," the Mother Superior unconsciously pushes Viridiana toward catastrophe. The curé of *La Mort en Ce Jardin* had this same kindness. "Kindness" (remember *Nazarín*, too) is a monstrosity, and "noble" motives can lead to results exactly the opposite of those anticipated.

In the Buñuelian world—of all worlds the most realistic because the most unexpected—everything is possible, even the consequence most at variance with human intentions.

So, in obedience to her Mother Superior, Viridiana arrives at her uncle's estate. He lives alone, neglecting his properties, and is cared for by a servant, Ramona, whom he took in some years earlier together with her little daughter.

As Don Jaime receives Viridiana, he says to her, "You will live here as you do in the convent." Then, wishing to show that he is as kind as the nuns, he saves a bee that is drowning in a tub of water.

All the uneasiness that already grips the novice is echoed in the phrase "as you do in the convent." That is to say, what does go on in the convent? Perhaps some day Buñuel will answer that question with another film—but does not Monk Lewis' *The Monk* already provide an answer?

In the uncle's gesture, we see again the fascination that insects have for Buñuel. His heroes destroy them in hate (*L'Age d'Or, Abismos de Pasión*), helplessly endure them (*Un Chien Andalou, L'Age d'Or, Las Hurdes*), egg them on to kill each other (*Robinson Crusoe*), or, ironically, refuse to kill them (*Ensayo de un Crimen*). All Buñuel's work belongs under the sign in the prologue of *L'Age d'Or*, does it not? The insect is a cold and terrible thing, the monster par excellence that may tomorrow become master of the world. Buñuel is closely related to Lautréamont.

One insect suffices to create atmosphere: unease enters and pervades the scene. One simple detail seemingly in no way connected with what is conventionally called the "action" enriches the

film first by its visual impact, which reinforces realism to the point of surrealism, and secondly by its disturbing appearance, which announces the manifold surprises to follow.

A subjective note: the attraction of insects is introduced instinctively, in an almost irrational way, and as a result the film advances to a higher level of meaning; it goes beyond the merely anecdotal and becomes the reflection of a complex, irradiant world.

To return to Don Jaime, whom we are beginning to know better. This still hale old man has a great secret. He had passionately loved his wife, who died of a heart attack on their wedding night before they had had time to make love. Like the hero of *El*, Don Jaime respected the marriage laws, and in consequence developed a pronounced neurosis. He has, it is true, one illegitimate son, whose existence he tries to ignore because he was born of a union unsanctified by the Church, but his one love experience has been disastrous. Ramona, his servant, is patently willing to sleep with him, but the old man cannot even conceive of such a liaison. He is reduced to eying the legs of her daughter as the little girl jumps rope, and to becoming aroused by trying on his dead wife's wedding gown. Voyeurism and masturbation, accordingly, are the elements of Don Jaime's sexuality, for all that he is a "noble," "believing," and "worthy" man.

Voyeurs are quite frequent in Buñuel's work; the hotel sequence in *El* is a minute analysis of the sickly dread of the voyeur. Don Jaime is more subtle. His motivation is no doubt unconscious when he presents the little girl with a new jumping rope that has one revealing characteristic: it has wooden handles, very phallic handles that the child must grip tightly as she jumps and twists and turns in a series of complicated maneuvers that make her socks slip down. The rope is a kind of Ariadne's thread that guides us through the entire film; we will meet it several times again.

Masturbation is present in *L'Age d'Or* (repetition of gesture, feathers, etc.) and is also one of the themes in *El* and *Robinson Crusoe*. In *Viridiana,* as, for that matter, also in *Robinson Crusoe* and in the first sequence of *Ensayo* it is complicated by transvesti-

tism and, as in *El, Ensayo,* and *Robinson Crusoe,* by a foot fetish.

Every evening Don Jaime opens a large trunk and takes out his wife's wedding gown and the other clothing that she was wearing when she died. To recapture her beloved image, he tries these garments on himself. He first puts on her high-heeled shoes, then her corset. Lacing the corset tightly, he goes to the mirror and looks at himself for a long time. Thus the boy in *Ensayo* puts on his mother's corset as a joke, before he discovers the erotic pleasure it gives him to look at his teacher's corpse. Thus Friday dresses up as a woman, which disturbs the prudish Robinson.

The legs and feet of women, and, by extension, their shoes, are a curious constant in Buñuel's films. The hero of *El* falls in love with a woman's feet; in *Ensayo,* a coquette puts her stocking on a gaming table; in *Susana* "respectable" people eye the feet of a "fallen'" girl. In *Viridiana,* the foot becomes even more obsessive than in *El.* Don Jaime plays the organ, and his feet, which we see in a close-up, are monstrous, for they are the same feet that he tries to slip into a woman's shoes.

The moment Viridiana arrives, her uncle notices her feet. His plans begin to take shape: the feet of the novice can wear the dead woman's shoes. For Don Jaime finds a strange resemblance between his niece and his dead wife. His niece must be, then, the wife who for him has never died.

The first day Viridiana spends on the estate is only outwardly calm. The novice has brought along all her religious paraphernalia —a heavy cross, a stone, a hammer, nails, and a crown of thorns. These assorted instruments of torture are among the surrealist elements to be found in several Buñuel films. Automatism and irrational enumeration are disturbing, especially when associated with a young and pretty woman. Is there a spectator who will not ask himself what the purpose of such objects may be? Are they customary in the convent? But, as I said earlier, let us await the film in which Buñuel will reveal convent life to us.

Viridiana arranges these instruments of piety and torture in her room. During the meal that follows, she indulges in the little game of peeling an apple with a single circular motion. Previously, in

the dream in *Subida,* the sustained peeling motion united variously the lovers and the son and the mother, thus becoming the umbilical cord.

I have no intention of explaining every detail in the film. On the contrary, in an instance such as the fruit peeling I am astonished by the irrational element that governs the sequence. I asked Buñuel about it, but he had forgotten even the existence of the peeling scene in *Subida* and had no idea why he used this detail at this particular point. This, then, is freedom in action; this is the constant intervention of imagination freed of all logical restraints in a work that never seeks to explain itself any more than we attempt to explain our own dreams while we are dreaming.

The second day the uneasiness mounts. The uncle wants to keep the girl with him. Finally he confesses his strange love, but only after he has asked the maid for help and she, devoted to him body and soul (Don Jaime feels no compunction in letting her understand that she is virtually his slave), is prepared to serve her master in everything.

So the servant is an accomplice; what is worse is that the old gentleman, finding himself in a dilemma, must demean himself by asking help from a person he despises. You will remember the hero of *El,* weeping before his valet, and the indifference of the guests in *L'Age d'Or* when confronted by the dramas that were taking place in the kitchen quarters.

While a spider's web is being spun around Viridiana, she is tasting for the first time the "wholesome joys of the country" and beginning to understand that everything on this earth will, in spite of herself, remind her that she is a woman. A farm hand is milking a cow, and suddenly she longs for a drink of milk. What more innocent desire? Yet the farm hand, no less innocent, urges her, "Try your hand at milking her!" "But—I don't know how!" "Try!" She kneels and reaches timidly for the teat. Now, a teat has a very definite form, and the hand of the novice does not dare, does not want to touch it.

The girl is a sleepwalker. She gets out of bed and, carrying a basket with knitting needles and wool, enters the room where Don Jaime listens endlessly to the Mozart Requiem. She throws

needles and wool into the fireplace and then scatters the ashes on her uncle's bed beside the dead wife's bridal wreath, which he has not had time to hide. This brief scene, resembling surrealist collages (a young girl in her nightgown enters an old man's bedroom and throws ashes on his bed), illustrates once again the working of Buñuel's mind, which is more than ever profoundly surrealist. Also, following on the scene with the teat, this erotic scene carries us still further into the unexpected.

Viridiana, who has previously indulged in a highly obscene strip tease (a nun's strip tease, after all!) when she discovers that under her supremely unfeminine garments—heavy stockings, coarse underwear—she is very beautiful, is not at all upset to learn on awakening that she has suffered a sleepwalking attack. "It happens to me at the convent, too." However, things are not so simple as they seem. She wants to leave and regain the safety of the convent in whose familiar waters she can move about without creating problems for herself. The uncle cannot prevent it, so he begs her to do him one last favor—to wear her aunt's gown. Viridiana is shocked, but she gives in to an old man's "harmless" caprice. He, in the presence of Ramona, pays fervent court to this dual woman. He finally confesses his deepest desire and asks her to marry him—or, rather, Ramona acts as intermediary and puts the question for him. Viridiana refuses, obviously. She starts to leave the room, the uncle calms her, asks her forgiveness, and Ramona pours the coffee that we know has been drugged. Viridiana falls asleep. Don Jaime picks up her inert body, dismisses Ramona (who goes looking for her daughter), and carries Viridiana to the bed.

Ramona's little daughter is upset. She has seen "the big black bull come in through the ceiling." In a film in which all the characters are poetic, this girl is the most poetic of all. She, more than any of the others, represents Buñuel. Like him, she is afraid of animals who become mythical creatures: the giraffe (*L'Age d'Or*), the mangy dog (*Subida, Los Olvidados*), the cocks (*Los Olvidados, El Bruto*), the pigeon (*Los Olividados, Viridiana*), the tortoise (*Cela S'Appelle l'Aurore*), not to mention all the animals of *Las Hurdes, Nazarín, La Mort en Ce Jardin*, etc. They comprise a

disturbing bestiary. They are portents, harbingers of trouble and catastrophe. The black bull of the girl's imagination hovers over the house of Don Jaime. Ramona's daughter, more curious than her mother, wants to see the bull and to find out what he has brought with him. So she climbs a tree and through the window watches Don Jaime worshiping the unconscious body of Viridiana.

The kiss he gives the young woman in the wedding gown recalls the orchestra leader's kissing Lya Lys (*L'Age d'Or*) and the kissing of the dead woman in *Abismos de Pasión*.

The uncle's eyes devour his niece. First the feet, of course; then he opens her bodice and looks at her breasts; finally he falls upon her but at the last moment restrains himself from rape. Did he renounce making love to his wife in the same way, when he saw that she was dead?

The next day, however, he believes he has an unanswerable argument that will keep Viridiana on the estate. He lies to her, pretending that he has raped her. The young woman feels the earth rock under her feet. She is no longer pure, she can no longer enter the convent. She runs blindly away, not caring where she goes.

She is about to board a bus when the authorities intercept her and take her back to the estate. "There's been an accident." Her uncle has killed himself. He has hung himself with the little girl's jumping rope—which the child quickly recovers despite the injunction that "a hangman's rope brings bad luck."

With this, the first part—or, rather, the prologue—of the film ends.

Viridiana cannot return to the convent. Convinced that she has been raped and believing herself (rightly, for that matter) the cause of her uncle's suicide, she feels corrupted. Her faith, however, is strong; like Nazarín, she wants, even outside the Church, to continue to be a Christian. She is now beyond the boundaries of what one could call clericalism and has little or nothing to do with "the true Christian vocation."

As he moves her out of an official religious context, Buñuel un-

consciously casts about for a difficulty. Everyone (even the fiercest champions of the Roman Church) attacks external aspects of religion—erring curés, erring flocks, even errant rites—but this is done in order the better to defend the essence of religion.

Christianity—in this, like any well-established religion—is a vast enterprise of coercion, the purpose of which is the defense of the established social and moral order. Channeling the people's need for the miraculous, it contributes brilliantly to the maintenance of that order at whatever cost.

Since this is an inadmissable objective, since the Pope cannot say, "Pray so that you will forget about going out on strike," religion hides its bloodstained hands (witness the wars of religion, the Inquisition, etc.) in gloves of immaculate whiteness. These gloves bear high-sounding names—pity, charity, Christian love, renunciation.

"Pure" spirits see only the gloves, never imagining that inside them are murderous fingers, and they serve the gloves, not knowing that they are thus fortifying the hands. Still purer spirits want blindly to carry out all the orders given by the gloves, eliminating, knowingly or not, the hands that animate them. But gloves without hands are lifeless casings, and any directions they give are lifeless, too.

The hands of religion drive Viridiana out, as Nazarín was driven out, and she thereupon seizes upon the gloves as if they were invested with a life of their own. As a result, while the novice renounces her vows, she does not give up being a Christian. She installs herself in one of the detached buildings on the estate, and when the worried Mother Superior comes to find out what has happened to her, she refuses to tell her real reasons for isolating herself and giving up the monastic life forever. The exasperated Mother Superior insists: 'You must tell me everything. I order you to tell me." To no effect. The hand is withdrawn, the glove remains. The separation is complete.

Hypocrites aside, no one dares defend the bloody hand of religion. Let us now see how the immaculate glove can defend itself alone. (I was right to say that Buñuel is looking for a difficulty.)

Like Lizardi, Nazarín, and the naïve curé in *El,* Viridiana is moved by all the great Christian precepts that weave the fabric of the gloves, and she wants to do good. In a nearby village she gathers up beggars, tramps, cripples, various old people, a blind man, and a leper, and she installs them in a part of her uncle's house, where she now lives, hoping to "save" them.

Jorge, the illegitimate son of Don Jaime, also arrives, accompanied by a rather ordinary young woman who is his current mistress. He is the sole heir, and so comes as master of the estate.

Jorge is an architect. It seems that for Buñuel this profession represents a kind of security, a mental well-being, a way of thinking that is stripped of poetry, a materialism not far removed from rationalism. Jorge resembles the young man who is so concerned about time toward the end of *Le Chien Andalou,* and especially the architect Raoul, in *El.* In other circumstances, he would also resemble the anarchist, Marchal, in *La Mort en Ce Jardin.* Jorge is never in doubt about anything. For that matter, he does not think much; he possesses the common sense that is so contrary to the "no-sense" of the monsters. He differs from the neurotics and exalted poets who are Buñuel's real heroes. Jorge is also "healthy" and therefore "good," but not to excess, just as he is "bad," but, again, not to excess. He is normal. He is a man who loves to be alive, to eat, to drink, to make love, but he is incapable of great passion.

The new master is amused by Viridiana's "whims." He is also very much attracted by her but is quickly discouraged. Making advances to a slightly touched mystic is a waste of time, the more so since he must busy himself about the estate. He launches various projects to clear the land and restore the big house. Being a practical man, he wants to make this capital that has fallen into his lap turn a profit for him.

To Viridiana he comes as a great surprise. There are, then, such coarse spirits who boast of their lack of faith, who admit that they offend against moral laws. Still, she accepts him, almost forgives him, for is she not a Christian? And, in any case, she must busy herself with her derelicts.

They are all monsters—not only the dwarf and the blind man,

and not only in a physical sense. They are monsters because, like Nazarín's prison companions, they represent "evil."

Note that when in a Buñuel film we meet "good" (Viridiana, for example) or "evil" (her protégés) this does not mean what it means in the films of other people because for Buñuel absolute good and absolute evil are beguiling, impassioning monstrosities. Buñuel loves Viridiana the pure as well as her impure wards. Were the world composed only of Jorges, it would not be viable, for in this child of nature the two elements of good and evil do not coexist; indeed, they are lacking altogether. Dr. Jekyll is a remarkable person, as Mr. Hyde is, also, and doubtless their coexistence would have produced a genius, a dual monstrosity—perhaps perfection.

We come here, I think, to the essential in all Buñuel's work. With a miraculous serenity, this extraordinary man, who is so drawn by the unusual and the rare, achieves a major synthesis, uniting in his hatred all that is mediocre and uniting in his love all that is exceptional and shocking, all that threatens to rock the foundations of our everlastingly tedious way of thinking, our shoddy way of living. He loves all these monsters, never forgetting that some monstrosities are more necessary than others. Thus he has the poor priest Lizardi killed by a mystical madman. He saves Nazarín by infecting his mind with doubt. He will save Viridiana by hurling her into the midst of life.

Again let us not forget that Buñuel is a Spaniard, like Zurbarán, Goya, Lazarillo, like the dynamiters of the Civil War. He loves monsters; they are his children, even if because of their nature he prefers some to others, and even if he seeks to channel their monstrosity.

For Buñuel the true monsters, the ones whom he despises, are the men and women who are incapable of loving excessively, of being wrong and of revolting, always to excess; the men and women who are not really alive; the zombies we meet daily in the street, on the subway, everywhere, whom dutifully learned precepts and habits corrupt.

Buñuel is a humane man, with a genuine capacity for love, who is devoted to de Sade because de Sade was the same sort of man,

also capable of love and prepared to pay in his own person for his great rebellions. De Sade stands at the opposite pole from petty Nazi torturers or the bloody killer-heroes of cheap fiction, from small-time murderers or the promoters of genocide and the atomic-bomb droppers. De Sade was a liberator and he knew how to hate precisely because he was capable of love.

"I love all men, but I do not love the society that some of them have created!" Buñuel says, obviously meaning by "society" the whole contemporary moral and social order. He loves all his characters who do not represent that order, all the outsiders. With one exception: the blind. Buñuel once told a journalist that the only antipathetic character in *Viridiana* is the blind beggar. The beggar is hypocritical, evil, repugnant from every point of view; it is he, furthermore, who stands for Christ in a scene from the film that will be discussed presently.

In *L'Age d'Or,* Modot vengefully kicks a blind man; the blind man in *Los Olvidados* is an old lecher dreaming of revenge and denouncing the boys he exploits, like his confrere in *Lazarillo de Tormes.*

Except for the blind men, then, the troupe that Viridiana wants to save is made up of men and women no worse than you or I. They are "evil" because that's the way they have turned out, because heredity and education drove them in that direction. Until they meet the young missionary, they have lived from hand to mouth, begging by the church door, maybe stealing here and there a bit of bread or a few pennies. They belong to the *Lumpenproletariat,* which is no longer capable of rebellion; they accept their situation and at the most grouse about it. They are the necessary reverse side of the gilded coin: the poor must exist so that the rich, as they come from Mass, can give them alms.

One of these beggars, however, sees that he will become a slave to Viridiana's complexes about kindness, and he does rebel. He wants to be free. After announcing his decision to his would-be benefactress, he has the further effrontery to ask her for a handout. This is the kind of sublime character one finds only in Buñuel. Here in a film of great violence is one simple detail invested with all the dignity and pride in the world. Here is someone who,

choosing to be free, dares mock his "benefactress" by forcing her to perform the ritual gesture of charity in behalf of someone who has just spat upon it.

Two servants on the estate presently display a similar dignity. They refuse to have anything to do with this strange asylum and go off, leaving Viridiana alone with her flock, while Jorge and his workmen labor nearby.

Viridiana's little "ideal society" gets itself organized, the tramps taking over the kitchen while the beggars work at whatever they have some aptitude for. The whole charming community works in the fields as well, for the queen of their kingdom believes that if she is giving them food and lodging, and especially if she is saving their souls, they should toil. Is this not how the Bible justifies man's exploitation of man?

Viridiana's protégés play along with consummate hypocrisy. Are they not all believers? "With all the troubles I've got, if I didn't have faith . . . !" one of them says. Only the leper finds it hard to be accepted as one of the group; being a Christian does not help anyone not to fear leprosy.

The leper deserves special attention. He has tried to cure himself with holy water. Results: negative. He feels alone. The others make him drag an old iron box behind him so that people can hear him approach. He chases some pigeons and catches one, which he hides inside his shirt. Without question, he is the most solitary figure in all Buñuel's work, not excepting Robinson Crusoe—and we know how powerfully obsessed by solitude Buñuel is. In *L'Age d'Or*, Modot throws white feathers out the window, and, in the same way, during the orgy that presently ensues, the solitary leper scatters the feathers of the pigeon he has undoubtedly already eaten. According to Freud's interpretation, feathers are a clear symbol of masturbation. You will remember that as a solitary Puritan Robinson rejects masturbation and, upon the arrival of Friday, also homosexuality. So solitude is one further form of the monstrous.

Viridiana, at last, is happy and full of smiles. "Her children" provide her with the opportunity to be a saint. She is the very

incarnation of charity, and great is her reward when at evening, in the fields, her chorus of tramps intone a ringing Angelus.

Here the cinemagraphic genius of Buñuel is again evident. Utilizing a parallel montage, he alternates the Angelus scenes with shots of the men working on the estate. Every time the tramps pronounce the name of God, the Virgin, or Christ, we pass without transition to shots of timber falling with a sinister crash, mortar being thrown on bricks, cement being mixed. The visual shock is extraordinary and, if one wishes, all possible revolutionary symbols can be seen in the contrast, but I think that the heavy accent on the holy names is sufficient.

Jorge, the rationalist, the unbeliever, is the hero of a fable that parallels the charitable efforts of Viridiana and that perfectly expresses Buñuel's intention. This is the fable of the dog and the cart.

At a certain point, a cart comes down the road. A mongrel dog is tied to the cart, which is rattling along apace, its good Christian owner being in a hurry to sell his merchandise. The exhausted dog is dragging its feet and seems on the verge of collapse, perhaps even of death. The upstanding young architect sees this scene, pities the dog, and speaks to the driver.

"You could put that poor dog in your wagon. He'll die if he has to go on like that."

"A dog doesn't belong in a wagon."

"Then unleash him, at least."

"No, he has to be leashed."

"Sell him to me!"

"I won't say no to that."

The transaction is quickly concluded, and Jorge goes off happily with his dog, who looks back at his old master with a certain regret. Jorge, very proud of himself for having saved one dog, does not see another wagon, identical to the first, coming from the opposite direction and dragging with it a dog even more spent than the first.

As a fable, this is far more instructive than all the foolishness of La Fontaine.

Jorge does not hesitate to tell Viridiana his opinion of her proj-

ect. What he cannot understand is why she has chosen the ugliest of all the beggars. He does not realize that the uglier the beggar, the more deserving of charity he is.

Soon Jorge's mistress becomes jealous of Viridiana and she leaves her lover, who promptly finds consolation by going to bed with the maid, Ramona. Jorge bears no resemblance to his father; he is one to take advantage of every opportunity that comes his way, he lives by exploiting everything. As I have said before, he is an atrociously normal man.

But the drama is not slow to explode. The fine Christian order Viridiana has established collapses.

I use the word "drama" ironically, since before going further I must emphasize the fact that *Viridiana* is a comedy or, in any case, a comic film. Buñuel's humor—macabre, obviously—is present in every shot. It has never been more searing than at the end of *Viridiana*.

Ramona's little daughter has to have a tooth pulled in the village, and her mother goes with her. Jorge must go with Viridiana to a notary to sign some papers. The beggars find themselves sole masters of the estate.

The tramps begin by inspecting rooms that until then had been closed to them, and quite soon they are rifling the drawers for luxurious table linens. A lamb is slaughtered, and the company assembles, "like the masters," around the large dining table for a feast. Only the leper sits apart.

Soon, with the help of wine, this splendid banquet turns into an orgy. There is much storytelling and rolling under the table, until one of the women has an amusing inspiration. She will immortalize the scene by taking a photograph with, she specifies, an old camera that her parents had given her, which still works.

In grouping themselves, they reproduce as if by chance da Vinci's "Last Supper." The blind man, the one evil man in the film, is none other than Christ; the cripples, the dwarfs, and the leper are the apostles.

No sooner have they struck this pose than we hear the stentorian crowing of a cock (again a cock, and here all the more disturbing because he also crows in the Bible). The woman who is to take

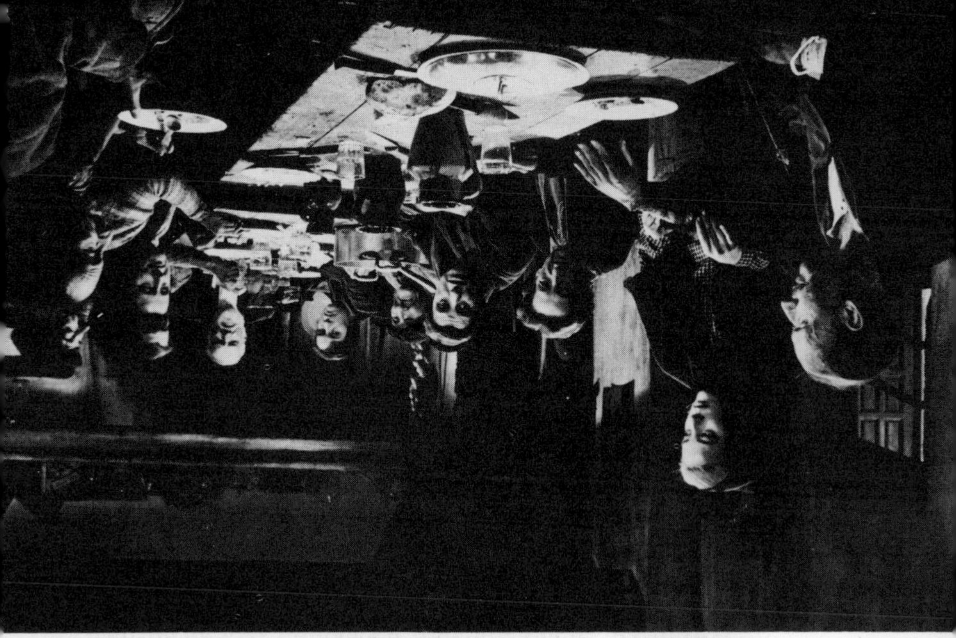

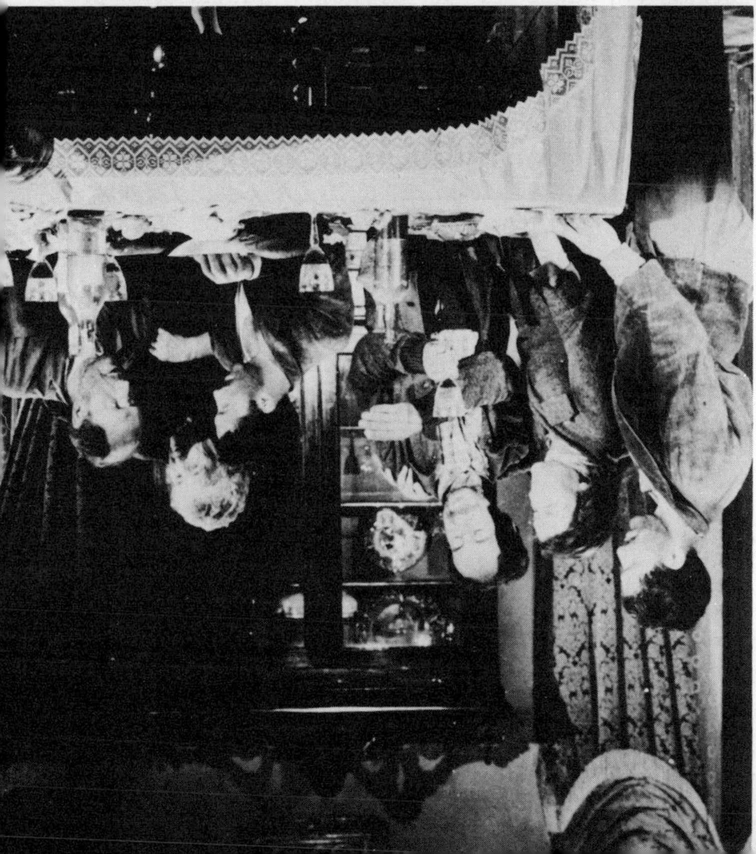

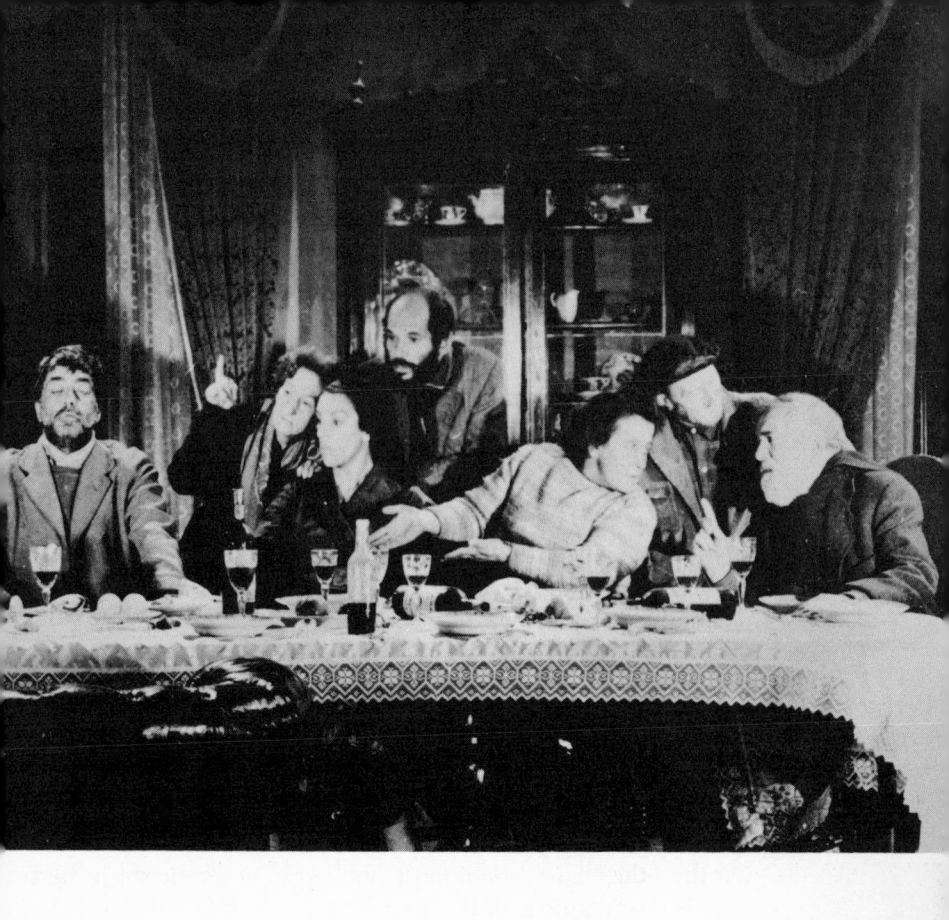

Scenes from *Viridiana*

the photograph moves in front of the table and, in an utterly obscene gesture, lifts her skirts.

Not since the ending of *L'Age d'Or* has Buñuel achieved so free a sequence. Everything about it is great, incredible, marvelously simple.

There are incorrigibles, I know, who insist that blasphemy is the token of great piety, that one must believe in order to want to destroy what one believes, and such nonsense. But let us be serious. Let us suppose that we were to say that every man, every Christian who does not blaspheme, is depriving himself of that pleasure because in his heart of hearts he does not believe. The great atheists, in this case, would be Claudel, Mauriac, the Pope. . . . How easy it is to reverse specious arguments! Or to put it another way: Would an old-line Communist who had been tortured under the czars have no right to curse the memory of his torturers without being accused of being secretly pro-czarist?

Furthermore, I must repeat that Buñuel is no longer trying to be blasphemous. He very serenely and simply offers us violent, hilarious images. As any psychoanalyst can explain, everyone's freely associated images are conditioned by the individual's childhood and education, especially if one has fought, rejected, conquered, and gone beyond those early experiences.

On the other hand, the almost pornographic eroticism in blasphemy is characteristic of the Spanish spirit. Let us not forget that the richest, most splendid oaths are Spanish.

The tramps' orgy is made up of little Goya-like tableaux. The violence of these scenes seems to me unique in the history of the cinema. Misshapen bodies copulate behind a handsome divan. "You have to do a lot of sinning to be able to do a good job of repenting," one of the beggars says. They empty Don Jaime's trunk, dance to the Mozart Requiem, which someone has put on the gramophone. The female dwarf, the cripples, and the leper dress up in the bridal gown and veils of Don Jaime's dead wife. Others, too drunk to stand up, sit and admire: "You would call it *Ecce Homo.*"

An informer tells the blind man that the beggar woman he occasionally sleeps with is making love at that very moment with

another man, and the jealous blind man wrecks everything in reach with his cane. The vast room, through which the Requiem still sounds, is now a sordid shambles.

At this point, Viridiana, Jorge, Ramona, and the little girl arrive home. The latter two run back to the village for help, while the cousins enter the house in time to see the heroes of this memorable dinner stagger away as fast as they can. The blind man gets entangled in the bride's veil.

The leper and one other man remain alone in the bedroom of the late Don Jaime to receive Jorge and Viridiana. Their reception is rather special, for while the leper attacks and binds Jorge, the other man, who is wearing the little girl's jumping rope as a belt, tries to rape Viridiana.

This second near-rape is much more than just an attempt, for even if the beggar does not achieve his purpose, Viridiana, who is wide awake this time, finally learns the nature of the carnal act. Buñuel underlines this very precisely: in her struggle, the young woman seizes the handles of her attacker's improvised belt with both hands. And so the circle is complete: the uncle gives the jumping rope to the little girl so that he can watch her dance, he hangs himself with it when his erotic dreams become unattainable, and through the same rope Viridiana encounters sex.

Jorge regains consciousness and, to save Viridiana from her attacker, bribes the leper, who is standing by, waiting his turn: "Perhaps when he's finished he'll pass her on to me." The lust for money is even stronger than sexuality; the leper kills his friend with a fireplace shovel and frees Viridiana.

Only then do the police arrive.

Once order has been restored, there remains the epilogue. It is made up of two sequences, both high points in Buñuel's achievement.

Having seen the consequences of her charity and having, to a degree, known a man, Viridiana feels lost. Who was she? Who is she? Her religious paraphernalia, like her dress, have become meaningless.

One evening, we find the little girl sitting before a wood fire.

She is playing with Viridiana's crown of thorns. The object intrigues and amuses her, but one of the thorns pricks her finger and she throws the crown into the fire.

Is there any sight more beautiful than a burning crown of thorns? The child is wonderstruck; she takes a stick and pulls the crown from the fire, the better to watch it burn.

Here again Buñuel's immense tenderness breaks through. The little girl is beauty itself; she is all purity, all poetry. She has not yet been destroyed by middle-class morals and prohibitions; she is still capable of appreciating the sublime image of the burning crown. If there is a symbol beyond this image, so much the better, but I am sure that for Buñuel it is merely the power of the image, the rest being instinct. The great revolutionary poems are like that—for example, those of Lautréamont and Rimbaud.

The second part of the epilogue offers some hints about Viridiana's future.

The original ending of the film had shocked the Spanish censor, who insisted that Buñuel find an alternative. The first version had Jorge and Ramona playing *belote,* and it is clear that they have just made love. Viridiana arrives, bewildered and haggard. Not knowing what to do or where to turn, she comes to see the man who can offer her the many marvelous things that she is only now beginning to glimpse. Delighted with this windfall, Jorge dismisses Ramona and closes the door behind her. The maid spies through the keyhole.

Spanish censorship winced. This was impossible; the public would perfectly well understand that Jorge and Viridiana were making love. Never! This must be changed. So Buñuel changed it, with the result that a felicitous but fairly tame ending became sublime.

Nothing is altered up to the point where Viridiana arrives, but then Jorge does not send Ramona away. He invites Viridiana to sit down, and the three of them, good companions all, play a hand of *belote.* Jorge has the last line in the film: "I knew very well that one day we would all play a little game together."

All this takes place to the accompaniment of a crude rock 'n'

roll record that Jorge has put on the phonograph. So, a film that opened musically with Handel's Hallelujah Chorus, which is played during the credits, ends with rock 'n' roll. The whole evolution of *Viridiana* follows the sound track. The Mozart Requiem serves as the sound background for the erotic follies of the uncle and the Hallelujah Chorus for the beggars' orgy, but for the "little game" *à trois*, we have rock 'n' roll.

Viridiana has discarded the trappings of holiness to move out into life, beginning with something that could not be flatter or more humdrum, a little game of cards.

Such is the destiny of saints who recognize how inane is their sanctity. Perhaps Viridiana will be saved—and on this point the film ends, for Viridiana no longer interests Buñuel unless, rescued from religion, she someday becomes a monster of another sort— a sublime monster, perhaps, and no longer a ridiculous or merely moving one. Maybe she will become a great lover or a revolutionary. For the moment, our heroine has moved into the prevailing order; she learns to play *belote*, and she plays with the man who will certainly go to bed with her.

Other Buñuel characters have completed their cinematic (but not their human) destiny in the same fashion, for creating points of suspension is one of Buñuel's great strengths—for instance, Francisco in the monastery (*El*), or, even earlier, Modot throwing the feathers of solitude out the window (*L'Age d'Or*). And is not the calm that is re-established after the arrest in *Susana* similar, and the cure in *Ensayo de un Crimen* equally ambiguous?

In *Viridiana* Buñuel has given us his most fully realized work in that it is the most freely personal. The government officials were not wrong when they banned the film in Spain, even forbade any mention of it in the press, and fired the censorship employee responsible for allowing this affront to religion to pass. And let us not speak of the articles in the Catholic press, and the *mea culpas* of the simpletons who dared claim that *Nazarín* was a Christian film.

BUÑUEL: A FREE SPIRIT

And tomorrow, what? We can expect a great deal from Buñuel's next films. Perhaps now he will be able to carry out one of the various projects that are close to his heart. Some of these are:

Illégible Fils de Flûte: A picaresque scenario, revolutionary and quite mad, written in collaboration with the Spanish poet Juan Larrea;

Siméon le Stylite: A reconstruction, only very slightly historical, of the life of this monstrous saint. One of the more unbiblical images he hopes to use is that of a pillar down the length of which Siméon's excrement flows, as wax flows down a candle. There is also an apparition of the Devil appearing in the guise of a six-year-old girl trundling a hoop.

Le Moine: This is based on Monk Lewis' novel, *Ambrosio, or The Monk.* What more Buñuelian subject is there?

And, finally, the remarkable *Naufragés de la Rue de la Providence,* which Buñuel wrote with his old friend Alcoriza, and which he hopes soon to film, thanks to the producer of *Viridiana,* who—miracle of miracles!—leaves him completely free.

Buñuel's work is inscribed in the history of the cinema in letters of fire because it is fiercely personal.

As indifferent to threats as to ill-intentioned praise, Luis alone continues to offer us a defense against commercialism, stupidity, falsehood, traditional logic, resignation. If today he holds a place that he has won with great difficulty, if he has an audience, it is because he alone gives expression to our desire—a desire that is becoming daily more universal—for a radical change in our way of thinking and in our way of living; because he is a magnificently untamed creature who dares dynamite the bars of our age-old prisons and teach us to look without being blinded upon the black sun.

He has attained this position because, before being a film man,

he is, quite simply, a man; because he is able to introduce his dreams into reality; because each time a bomb explodes somewhere in the world, killing innocent people, he suffers; because he fights all forms of moral and social Nazism (he was among those who demonstrated against the execution of Sacco and Vanzetti); because he does not consider himself free so long as one single man on this earth suffers at the hands of others who think they are his masters; because he knows how to be a revolutionary, a surrealist; because he is a great and free spirit, strong enough to help us alter life and set man free.

The pieces in the remainder of this volume were selected by Ado Kyrou and Pierre Lherminier.

2. BUÑUEL ON THE CINEMA

REVIEWS

BATTLING BUSTER

WRITTEN AND DIRECTED BY BUSTER KEATON

[*Cahiers d'Art*, No. 10, 1927]

A wonderful film. Aseptic. Disinfectant. The blinders of tradition are cast off, and our eyes grow bright again as we watch Buster's young-hearted, balanced world. Here is a great specialist in treating the disease called sentiment. His film is great; it's like a good bathroom; it has the vitality of an Hispano. Buster will never try to make us tearful; he knows that the too-quick tear is finished and done with. On the other hand, he is no clown trying to make us roll in the aisles. Yet we do not stop smiling for a moment—we smile not at him but at ourselves, and it is a smile of health and Olympian strength.

In the area of the cinema, I will always put the characteristically melancholy expressiveness of a Keaton above the endlessly nuanced expressions of a Jannings. Film makers misuse Jannings; they multiply the slightest contraction of his facial muscles to the nth degree. With Jannings, grief is a prism with a hundred faces. That is why he can perform on a screen a hundred and fifty feet wide and if asked for "just a little more," will manage to show us that on the strength of his face alone an entire film could be made and called "The Jannings Expression, or, A Study of X Wrinkles, Photographed from A to A."

Buster Keaton's expression is as simple as a bottle's, although we can always detect his aseptic spirit dancing around the clear circle of that unblinking eye. A bottle and the face of Buster Keaton can express infinite points of view.

Few of us are able, as he is, to achieve while we work that rhythmic and archetectonic meshing which is a film. Editing is the

key; editing combines, comments on, and unifies all the elements. Can one possibly achieve more cinemagraphically? Yet some people think Keaton—the antivirtuoso—inferior to Chaplin. The rest of us consider it vastly to his credit that Keaton achieves his purpose by working directly with all the means of comic expression. Keaton is full of a humanity quite beyond a recent, uncreated brand of what one might call fashionable humanity.

There is much talk about technique in films like *Metropolis*, *Napoléon*, etc. No one ever mentions the technique of films like *Battling Buster*, and that is because here technique is so indissolubly fused with all other elements that people are not even aware of it. In much the same way, we live in a house without ever thinking of the potential durability of its materials. The superfilms should serve as lessons for technicians; the films of Keaton can enlighten reality itself, with or without the realistic technique.

The Jannings school: European; sentimental; biased in favor of art and literature; traditional; John Barrymore, Veidt, Mosjouskine, etc.

The Keaton school: American; vital; photogenic; lacking culture and tradition; Monte Blue, Laura LaPlante, Bebe Daniels, Tom Moore, Adolphe Menjou, Harry Langdon, etc.

NAPOLÉON BONAPARTE
WRITTEN AND DIRECTED BY ABEL GANCE
[*Cahiers d'Art*, No. 3, 1927]

It seems to me that Northern peoples have an innate gift for the art of the film whereas we Latins, burdened by our particular tradition, mysticism, culture, and inspiration, are responsive transmitters for other forms of art but are powerless to assimilate the art of the cinema. Every attempt we make only confirms the superiority of young societies over our own.

American films have been much criticized for being, in general, trivial. However, any one of them, no matter how modest, is always sincere—even if primitively so—and completely photogenic and totally cinemagraphic in rhythm.

The Americans let us see the essence of the drama (actually, this is only secondary). When they hit upon some happy device, they never abuse it, for it is in their nature to be forever forging ahead to something new. They unquestionably possess a far more evolved film sense than we.

Many cultivated people have an a priori prejudice against the seventh art, of course, but they also are borne along by the currents of the times and would, I think, welcome any serious film endeavor. What is needed is a film that would open their eyes to the manifold potentialities of the medium. Taking perhaps at face value the fulsome praise that our foremost critics heaped on *Napoléon,* the skeptics went to see it—and you can imagine what they thought.

Gentlemen, we should say to them, this is not cinema. This is anticinema. Go see *The Ingénue* instead. It's an American film about an amorous Amazon, which ends with a single chaste kiss. But it is light, fresh, and brimming with cadenced images that have been composed by a genuinely cinematic imagination.

COMMON CLAY

DIRECTED BY VICTOR FLEMING

[*Cahiers d'Art,* No. 10, 1927]

Technique is a quality no less essential to a film than to any other work of art or even to an industrial product. It is a mistake to suppose, however, that technique determines a film's excellence. A film may have qualities other than technique that interest us more. The public, remember, does not waste time analyzing the technical methods used in making a film; generally, it asks nothing more than that the film be emotionally appealing. But true emotion is not to be confused with lachrymose sentimentality. All things considered, Victor Fleming's film is devoid of authentic emotion and is therefore a counterfeit film. While it is technically excellent, like many other films it stimulates our tear ducts far

more than our sensibilities. You can positively hear the teardrops falling throughout the theater. Everybody watching *Common Clay* discovers that he can sniffle with the best.

Why don't we adopt the practice of submitting films to a minute microscopic examination before they are shown publicly? The microscope is the indicated instrument. Had this method been applied to the Fleming film, it would surely have shown that the movie is ridden with germs of melodrama, consumed by sentimental typhus, and that wide areas of the corpus are infected by romantic and naturalistic bacillae.

We had supposed the cinema immune by now to such epidemics. Still, if it takes a poison to counter a poison, it takes a film to counter a film.

POETRY AND CINEMA

[TEXT OF AN ADDRESS DELIVERED AT THE UNIVERSITY OF MEXICO IN 1953]

Octavio Paz said once that "A chained man need only shut his eyes to make the world explode." Paraphrasing him, I would say that the white eye of the screen need only reflect the light that is properly its own to blow up the universe. But, for the time being, we can sleep easily, for the cinemagraphic light that reaches us is carefully filtered and metered. In none of the traditional arts is there so great a disproportion between potential and achievement as in the cinema. A film acts directly upon the spectator, presenting him with concrete people and things; in the silence and darkness of the theater, it isolates him from what we might call his normal psychic habitat. For these reasons, it can stimulate him more effectively than any other form of human expression. It can also more effectively stultify him. The bulk of current film production seems, unfortunately, to have this as its mission, and the screens of our film houses daily parade evidence of the moral and intellectual void in which the cinema is wallowing. The fact is that the cinema limits itself to imitating the novel or the stage—but with this difference:

that as a medium it is less richly endowed with the means of psychological expression. It is repeating *ad nauseam* the same old stories that the nineteenth century had already wearied of telling but that nonetheless drone on in the modern novel.

A moderately cultivated man would toss aside a book based on any one of the subjects that make up the plots of our biggest films. Yet that same man, comfortably seated in a dark theater, is dazzled by a light and movement that exert an almost hypnotic power over him; he is fascinated by the faces of people and by the rapid shifts of scene, so that he placidly accepts the film bromides, no matter how stale.

The filmgoer is robbed of an important share of his critical faculties by this lulling influence. I will give one concrete example —*Detective Story.* The structure of the story is perfect; the director is excellent, the actors exceptional, the production original. But all this talent, all this know-how, all the complicated steps involved in producing a film have been devoted to a story that in content is both stupid and remarkably low in moral caliber. It makes me think of that extraordinary machine in *Opus 11:* it is a gigantic apparatus made of the finest grade of steel; it has a thousand complex gears, tubes, manometers, levers; it is engineered as precisely as a watch, but on the scale of an ocean liner; its sole function is to postmark the mail.

The essential element in any work of art is mystery, and generally this is lacking in films. Authors, directors, and producers take great pains not to disturb our peace of mind, and they keep the marvelous window of the screen closed to the liberating world of poetry. They would rather have that screen reflect subjects that could perfectly well be sequels to our everyday life; they prefer that it repeat over and over the same hackneyed drama to make us forget the tedium of our daily work. Their approach is, of course, sanctioned by conventional morality, official censorship, and religion; it is ruled by good taste, and seasoned with an innocuous humor together with all the other prosaic imperatives of reality.

Anyone who is eager to see good films will rarely be satisfied by the big expensive productions or by those that have won criti-

cal praise or wide popular acceptance. The personal story, the private individual drama, cannot, in my opinion, interest anyone who is truly alive to the contemporary world. If the spectator shares in the joys, sorrows, and anguish of a character on the screen, it can only be because he sees in that character the reflection of the joys, sorrows, and anguish of society as a whole and, by extension, his own. Unemployment, the instability of society, the fear of war, and so on—these are the things that affect all men today and, accordingly, they affect the spectator. But that Mr. So-and-So is not happy at home and casts about for a girl friend to provide him some fun, and that he then abandons her to return to his self-sacrificing spouse—all this is unquestionably moral and edifying but it leaves us completely indifferent.

Sometimes that which is the essence of cinema springs unexpectedly from an otherwise insipid movie—a slapstick comedy, or a banal romantic film. Man Ray once said something very significant: "The worst movies I've ever seen in my life, the kind that put me sound asleep, always have five minutes that are marvelous. But the best, the most highly praised films, have barely five minutes that are even worthwhile." What this means is that in all films, good or bad—and beyond and despite the intentions of directors—cinematic poetry struggles to come to the surface and reveal itself.

In the hands of a free spirit the cinema is a magnificent and dangerous weapon. It is the superlative medium through which to express the world of thought, feeling, and instinct. The creative handling of film images is such that, among all means of human expression, its way of functioning is most reminiscent of the work of the mind during sleep. A film is like an involuntary imitation of a dream. Brunius* points out how the darkness that slowly settles over a movie theater is equivalent to the act of closing the eyes. Then, on the screen, as within the human being, the nocturnal voyage into the unconscious begins. The device of fading allows images to appear and disappear as in a dream; time and space become flexible, shrinking and expanding at will; chronological order and the relative values of time duration no longer corre-

* Jacques B. Brunius, a French writer.

spond to reality, cyclical action can last a few minutes or several centuries; shifts from slow motion to accelerated motion heighten the impact of each.

The cinema seems to have been invented to express the life of the subconscious, the roots of which penetrate poetry so deeply. Yet it is almost never used to do this. Among modern film trends,* the best known is the so-called neorealism. The neorealistic film offers the spectator what seem to be moments from real life, involving real people caught as they move about the street, and having even authentic scenery and interiors. With some exceptions, among which I would single out *Bicycle Thief,* neorealism has done nothing to spark what is properly and characteristically cinematic—I mean the mysterious and the fantastic. What is the point of all the visual dressing up if the situations, the motives that animate the characters, their reactions, and even the plots themselves are drawn or copied from the most sentimental, conformist literature? The most worthwhile contribution—and it comes not from neorealism generally but from Zavattini specifically—is the raising of a humdrum act to the level of dramatic action. In *Umberto D,* one of the most interesting of the neorealistic films, an entire ten-minute reel is devoted to showing a maid go through a series of actions that only a short while ago no one would have considered worthy of being filmed. We see the maid go into the kitchen, light the fire, put on a casserole, throw water several times on some ants that are advancing Indian file across the wall, take the temperature of an elderly man who feels feverish. Despite the trivial side of the situation, we follow her movements with interest and even with a certain suspense.

Neorealism has introduced a few elements to enrich the language of cinematic expression, but nothing more. Neorealistic reality is incomplete, conventional, and above all, rational. The poetry, the mystery, all that completes and enlarges tangible reality, is utterly lacking. Neorealism confuses ironic fantasy with the fantastic and the grotesque.

"The most admirable thing about the fantastic," André Breton has said, "is that the fantastic does not exist; everything is real."

* This was said in 1953.—A.K.

I was talking with Zavattini some months ago, and I said to him that I was not in sympathy with neorealism. Since we were lunching together, the first illustration that came to mind was a glass of wine. For a neorealist, I said, a glass is a glass and nothing more. We see it being taken from the sideboard, being filled with wine, carried presently to the kitchen where the maid will wash it, or maybe she will break it, which will result in her being fired or in her not being fired, and so on. But this same glass, seen by different human beings, can be a thousand different things, because each person pours a certain dose of subjective feeling into what he is looking at, because no one sees things as they are but as his desires and his state of mind make him see them. I am fighting for the kind of film that will make me see this kind of glass, for it is this kind of cinema that will give me a total vision of reality, enlarge my knowledge of things and of people, and open to me the marvelous world of the unknown, of everything that I do not find in any newspaper or on any street.

Do not think from what I have just said that I am for a cinema exclusively dedicated to the expression of the fantastic and mysterious, for a cinema that flees from or despises daily reality and aspires only to plunge us into the unconscious world of dreams. A few moments ago I indicated all too briefly the capital importance I attach to the film that deals with the fundamental problems of modern man, and so I must emphasize here that I do not consider man in isolation, not as a single case, but in the context of his relationships with other men. I will let Friedrich Engels speak for me. He defines the function of the novelist (and here read film maker) thus: "The novelist will have acquitted himself honorably of his task when, by means of an accurate portrait of authentic social relations, he will have destroyed the conventional view of the nature of those relations, shattered the optimism of the bourgeois world, and forced the reader to question the permanency of the prevailing order, and this even if the author does not offer us any solutions, even if he does not clearly take sides."

INTERVIEWS (excerpts)

With André Bazin and Jacques Doniol-Valcroze

[*Cahiers du Cinéma*, June 1954]

BAZIN: In your opinion, what is the relationship between a film like *Las Hurdes* and your earlier work? What connection do you see between surrealism and documentary statement?

BUÑUEL: I think there is an important relationship between them. I made *Las Hurdes* both because I was concerned with the conditions of human existence and because I had a surrealist vision. I saw reality very differently from the way in which I would have seen it before surrealism. I was sure of that at the time, and so was Pierre Unik. . . .

For me *Los Olvidados* is a film about social struggle. Simply because I am, I think, honest with myself, I had to do a film of social significance. I know that I am moving in that direction. But aside from that, I did not want to make a polemical film. I observed things that moved me and I wanted to transpose those things onto the screen—but to do so with the love I have for the instinctive and the irrational that can reveal itself in anything and everything. I've always been drawn toward the strange and the unknown. . . .

The hero of *El* is a type that interests me, rather like a beetle or a malarial mosquito. . . . Insects have always fascinated me; I guess I am part entomologist. . . . The study of physical reality I find absorbing. . . .

For me it is natural to tend to see and to think of a situation from a sadistic* rather than from, say, a neorealistic or mystical point of view. I ask myself: What must this character reach for? A revolver? A knife? A chair? In the end, I always choose whichever is most disturbing. That's all. . . .

---

* See Mr. Kyrou's comment on Buñuel's attitude toward de Sade's work on page 89. It places this statement in its proper context.

I love moments in which nothing happens—when, for example, a man says, "Give me a light." That kind of thing interests me. "Give me a light" interests me enormously. Or "Do you want something to eat?" Or "What time is it?" I made *Subida al Cielo* more or less in this sense. . . .

Robinson [*Crusoe*] was suggested to me, just as my other film subjects have been. I didn't like the novel but I liked the character, and I agreed to do the film because there's a kind of purity in Robinson. In the first place, he's a man face to face with nature; there's no fictitious adventure, no elaborately contrived plot, no trite love scenes. Robinson is simply a fellow who lands on an island, finds himself at grips with primitive nature, and has somehow to manage to feed himself. The subject appealed to me, so I agreed to do the film, and I tried to do things that would be interesting. . . . I made it in the one way I knew how, wanting particularly to show man's solitude, the anguish of a man deprived of human society. I also wanted to deal with the subject of love—the lack of love or friendship, I mean, the dilemma of a human being without the companionship of man or woman. And in spite of the cuts, I think that the relationship between Robinson and Friday is still clear—the "superior" Anglo-Saxon and the "inferior" Negro. That is, Robinson is imbued with a sense of his own superiority and he's mistrustful, yet in the end they achieve the brotherhood of man; they meet each other proudly, like men! This was my intention, and I hope it's clear in the film. . . .

BAZIN: From what you've said, I see that you have kept some connections with surrealism—if not in an official or orthodox way, at least as a source of inspiration. You don't deny the influence of surrealism on your development; on the contrary, it's still vital and stimulating for you. Is that so?

BUÑUEL: I don't deny it in the slightest. Surrealism taught me that life has a moral meaning that man cannot ignore. Through surrealism I discovered for the first time that man is not free. I used to believe man's freedom was unlimited, but in surrealism I saw a discipline to be followed. It was one of the great lessons of my life, a marvelous poetic step forward. I haven't belonged to the group, however, for a long time. . . .

I don't like to go to the films but I love the film as a medium of expression. There is none better, I find, to show us a reality that we do not come in contact with every day of our lives. That is to say, through books, newspapers, and our own experience we come to know an exterior, objective reality. By its very mechanism, the cinema opens a little window for us on an extension of that reality. When I look at a film, my one wish is that it reveal something to me. It happens rather seldom. The rest doesn't interest me. I'm already too old. . . .

BAZIN: You told me . . . one day that thanks to Denise Tual you'd been able to see Robert Bresson's *Anges du Péché*, and that your chief recollection of this film was that of the nun whose feet were being caressed.

BUÑUEL: Ah yes, a very fine scene—and a very fine film!

BAZIN: I was a bit surprised, because this doesn't seem to me the most characteristic scene in *Anges du Péché*.

BUÑUEL: I see what you mean. . . . In actuality, I am not at all either sadistic or masochistic. I am so only theoretically. I accept sadism and masochism only as elements of struggle and of violence. Throughout Bresson's film I kept sensing something imminent, something that attracted me greatly, which unfolded in that final scene in an unquestionably disturbing way. That's why I remember only that a dead nun's feet were embraced. Having said this, I must add that personally I do not care to caress the feet of dead nuns or the feet of dry cows or any other foot, for that matter. . . . But here it was like the flowering of certain feelings that had been latent throughout the film. . . . I was in New York once for a meeting of the Association of Producers of Documentary Films, which was attended by the foremost young American film makers. There was a showing of *Las Hurdes*, and one of the Americans, full of enthusiasm, came up to me and asked how I'd got the wonderful idea of using Brahms's music. But I hadn't contrived anything special. I had simply found that the music of Brahms corresponded to the general spirit of the film. I used the Fourth Symphony—I remember that it was on four Brunswick records. Everyone was flabbergasted by a thing as simple—as silly, almost—as this, because everyone is always searching for effects and com-

plications. Personally, I don't like music in films; I think it's a lazy device, a kind of trickery—with some exceptions, naturally. At this festival, I was very much surprised to see some great films without music. I could name you three or four in which there were passages lasting twenty minutes or more without any music at all. *The Great Adventure,** for example. . . . Now I am deaf, so perhaps I just didn't hear; there may have been an eighty-piece orchestra playing all the time, but that's all the same to me and proves to my satisfaction that in any case silence would have been preferable. . . . I see that world-wide film production reflects the possibility of music's often being omitted. Silence! Ah, that's what is truly impressive! I've discovered nothing about music, but instinctively I think of it as a parasitical element which serves chiefly to make the most of scenes that otherwise have no cinematic interest.

With François de Montferrand

[*Radio, Cinéma, Télévision,* June 20, 1954]

When I asked Buñuel what he thought of the notion of the impossible film, he answered, as I expected he would, that the notion of the possible film is alien to him.

BUÑUEL: Except for the three surrealist films I directed from 1928 to 1932, I have never suggested a subject to a producer. I have directed only on commission. I've turned down subjects I thought were too bad and tried to salvage as best I could the ones I agreed to work on. Even films like *El* and *Robinson Crusoe* were done on order.

MONTFERRAND: But have you never thought of adapting a book you liked?

BUÑUEL: Oh yes. In 1932, I would have given anything to direct *Wuthering Heights,* which, as you know, is a novel that the surrealists discovered and claimed for their own. No producer would hear of it. Seven years later, in Hollywood, William Wyler made

---

* A Swedish documentary directed by Arne Sucksdorff.

it. Two years ago, a Mexican producer suggested that I direct my own version. Although I'd lost interest, I agreed. You'll soon be able to judge for yourself what it is worth.

MONTFERRAND: Well, I should have put the question differently and asked you this: Have you any possible film subjects you would like to direct?

BUÑUEL: The answer is no. Well, I can mention one film that I do dream about because I never will direct it. Basing my ideas on Fabre, I would invent characters as realistic as those in *Un Chien Andalou* or *L'Age d'Or,* but they would have the characteristics of insects. For example, the heroine would behave like a bee, the hero like a beetle, and so on.

MONTFERRAND: In a way then, it would be a film about the instinctual?

BUÑUEL: That's it. So you see why it's a hopeless project.

With François Truffaut

[*Arts,* July 21, 1955]

TRUFFAUT: You don't like your work to be taken too seriously, I believe. *La Vie Criminelle d'Archibaldo de la Cruz* [*Ensayo de un Crimen*] is, for you, just an amusing little film. And yet I've heard that at screenings your guests were very much taken with it—even rather frightened by it.

BUÑUEL: It's a comedy nonetheless. You must laugh at it, I assure you. I don't direct film on subjects of my own choosing; among several that may be proposed I select the one that convinces me and that I can rework. Conceivably, I may introduce some irrational elements—under cover of a dream—but never anything symbolic. I've heard or read interpretations of *Un Chien Andalou,* each more ingenious than the last, but all of them mistaken. Dali and I picked the gags—whatever occurred to us—and were merciless in throwing out everything that could mean anything. I've kept this taste for the irrational.

TRUFFAUT: People have surrounded you and your work with a

legend to the effect that Buñuel is a sadist, and so on, which is stupid. Still, it is true that you like to "disturb" to a point where one might almost say of you, as of Gide in his books, that you make films in order to disquiet people.

BUÑUEL: I do not try, it is true, to do anything that is either unworthy or reassuring. One must not make people believe that all is for the best in this best of all possible worlds. It is not necessary to destroy everything, to make subversive films, but I'd like *Pane, Amore, e Fantasia* [*Bread, Love, and Dreams*] better if it had a little less fantasy and a little less optimism. . . . I find that after five weeks I am bored with a film subject, and I really see no point in "living with" it for a long time. Once the scene has been sufficiently rehearsed, two or three takes of each frame are enough.

TRUFFANT: And yet, even from the technical point of view, your Mexican films are superior to most French films.

BUÑUEL: So? Well, technique is no problem for me. I have a horror of posed shots, and I detest unusual angles. Sometimes I work out with my cameraman what we think is a superbly clever perspective; everything is arranged down to the very last detail, and then when the time comes for shooting, we burst out laughing, throw the whole plan out, and simply shoot with no special camera effects.

TRUFFAUT: That's all very well, but the staging for *El, Subida al Cielo,* or *Archibaldo* is not at all conventional; quite the contrary, it is definitely invented—and very inventive.

BUÑUEL: Well, I dislike conventional staging, too—full frame, reverse shot, and all that. A director should not cover himself by filming a scene in several ways and then extricate himself from whatever difficulties arise by editing. I like long shots and perspectives with continuity. For example, I very much like Hitchcock's work in *The Rope.* If I shoot two hundred and fifty frames, there will be two hundred and fifty frames in my film. No duds, no additional overhead.

TRUFFAUT: The music in your films is always admirable.

BUÑUEL: Oh, dear! I detest music in films. I try to keep it out of my work because it makes for a too easy effect. How many films would stand up on their own if the music were omitted?

This much being said, I also like the music in my films. I directed *Abismos de Pasión* recently. Since this is a film that I wanted to do twenty years ago when I was a great Wagner fan, I put an hour's worth of Wagner into the film. But I allow music only when the scenario calls for it. I no longer tolerate background music to accompany a parade or to punctuate an embrace.

With Simone Dubreuilh

[*Les Lettres Françaises,* October 11, 1956]

BUÑUEL: I will direct an adaptation only if I think I shall be able at some point or other to express myself, to say something of my own, to slip myself in between two images. I have never yet sold myself. I do have to work and my job is directing films, but since *L'Age d'Or* I have never changed my moral principles. I say always and only those things that matter greatly to me. If I no longer say them exactly in the same way, that is because at fifty-five I can no longer think things exactly as I did at thirty. . . .

DUBREUILH: Aren't you going to direct *La Femme et le Pantin?*

BUÑUEL: Yes, when I've found the actress who can play the lead —a sensual, virginal, demonic little girl. I don't care at all for the surface eroticism in Pierre Loüys' work, which is so fashionable in films today—kissing, undressing, and all that. It shocks me. I am modest. So I blush. Furthermore, it's all external. What I will express is another kind of sensuality—a more profound, devouring, and terrible sensuality. I would like to make it the portrait of female perversity. . . . And yet it will be a film that can be seen even by children. I will not be "explicitly scandalous."

With Jean de Baroncelli

[*Le Monde,* December 16, 1959]

BARONCELLI: *Nazarín,* which won the special jury award at the 1959 Cannes Festival, has just been shown with great success at

Acapulco. According to the latest reports, it seems likely to capture the André Bazin prize. Now, as you know, there's been talk in connection with this film of your returning to Catholicism. What would you have to say about that?

BUÑUEL: Everyone is free to find in my films anything he likes or whatever is useful to him. Personally, when I read some of the comments I am dumfounded. Where do people go looking for the things they find to say? I love *Nazarín* because it is a film that allowed me to express certain things I care about. But I don't believe that I denied or abjured anything.

A flash of malice sparkled in Buñuel's eyes, and in his soft, persuasive voice he added: "I am an atheist still, thank God."

With Michèle Manceaux

[*L'Express*, May 12, 1960]

MANCEAUX: What is your attitude now toward the Catholic religion?

BUÑUEL: I have no attitude toward the Catholic religion. I was brought up in it. I could say this: I am still, thank God, an atheist. I believe that one must search for God in man. That is a very simple attitude.

With Manuel Michel

[*Les Lettres Françaises*, May 12, 1960]

BUÑUEL: Nowadays everyone is trying to lure the public with scenes of nakedness and sensuality. The middle-class public that swarms into the movie houses clamors for them as vociferously today as twenty or thirty years ago it condemned them. They are very easy to do, and to the extent that they correspond to the prevailing mentality, to make them means giving in to the prevailing conformism. But it hardly means giving up love. In *La Jeune*

Fille, Miller [the leading maie character], who is brutal by nature, shows a certain imagination in love. When he could have been violent with the young girl, Ewie, he acts almost against his own nature: he is tender, he gives her gifts, he falls in love. Nevertheless, his relationship with Ewie is unequivocal and for that reason there was no need to prove it by a plethora of "daring" scenes.

With Guy Allombert

[*Image et Son,* October 1960]

BUÑUEL: I put into my films what I want to put into them. But no more dreams! I have enough dreams to be able at this point to plagiarize myself, and I have no wish to remake films I've already made. Perhaps I might like to remake an *Olvidados* or an *El*—or an updated *L'Age d'Or.* . . . But what I ask of the cinema is that it bear witness, that it be a statement about the world, that it say everything that is important about what is real. . . .

With Elena Poniatowska

[*Revista de la Universidad de Mexico,* January 1961]

BUÑUEL: I was Jean Epstein's assistant and he was my teacher. I collaborated with him on *Mauprat,* in 1927. But as early as the third and last film I made with him—the French version of *The Fall of the House of Usher*—I had already become half surrealist, although at first I'd made fun of the surrealists and didn't take them seriously. All the same, at the time of this third film, when I was Epstein's assistant, I was already flirting with surrealism. . . . One day Epstein told me he had loaned the Epinay studio, where we were working, to Abel Gance, who would be coming out to make a little experiment. "Help him out if he needs you," he told me. It was normal that as Epstein's assistant I should be available

to Gance if he were to want me, but I refused: "Let him hire his old mother if he needs an assistant," or words to that effect. Epstein stared hard at me for a moment and said, "Buñuel, my friend, you and I have come to a parting of the ways." I will always remember what he said to me when I tried to explain: "I'm happy to be your assistant, to work for you. But Gance, out of the question. Gance doesn't interest me in the slightest." And Epstein answered, "That a little turd like you dare speak like that about a great personality like Gance!" Then he added: "So much for that. We will not work together any more. I'll drive you back to Paris." (I had no way of getting about and Epinay is way out of town.) On the drive back, he advised me to stay away from that iconoclast surrealist group; his last words to me were that I should stay clear of them, and I followed his advice to the letter—so closely that one year later I joined them. I was really more interested in surrealism than in finishing the film, and Epstein completed it alone. I plunged into surrealism with Salvador Dali and made my first film, *Un Chien Andalou.*

I financed the film myself, or rather, my mother paid for it. I was the "new wave" of that day, and I made the film because my mother sent me five thousand duros—about a hundred and forty thousand francs at the time.

PONIATOWSKA: You'd had some preparation before you started directing the film? You'd studied, I suppose?

BUÑUEL: Good heavens, no! No! Nothing of the sort. Before that I went to dance halls and did a lot of silly things. . . .

When *Un Chien Andalou* was shown for the first time, I was prepared for a public uproar and stuffed my pockets full of stones, just in case. I stayed behind the screen and tended to the phonograph. I put on a passage from *Tristan,* then an Argentine tango, then *Tristan* and tango, *Tristan* and tango, tango and *Tristan,* through to the end. I was peering out at the audience to see what the reaction would be, but the only people who came were aristocrats and artists, and among them they filled the three or four hundred seats at the Ursulines. Le Corbusier was there, and the kind of people who were reading—or writing for—*Cahiers d'Art.* The enormous enthusiasm *Un Chien Andalou* aroused in them

stunned me. When the showing was over, they got up and clapped and clapped. Those stones weighed pretty heavily in my pockets. I was puzzled—but pleased, really. . . .

PONIATOWSKA: They say that before *Los Olvidados* you made some pretty run-of-the-mill films.

BUÑUEL: Yes. There was *Gran Casino*, with Jorge Negrete and Libertad Lamarque. . . . But I always followed my surrealist principle: the necessity of eating never excuses the prostitution of art. Out of nineteen or twenty films, I have three that are frankly bad, but in not one case did I compromise my moral code. To many people a personal code is a childish thing, but not to me. I am against conventional morality—all our traditional illusions, sentimentality, and the moral filth of society that is engendered by sentimentality. Obviously, I have made some bad films, but they have always been morally decent.

PONIATOWSKA: What do you mean by morality?

BUÑUEL: Morality—middle-class morality, that is—is for me the *im*moral, which one must fight. It is the morality that is founded on our most unjust social institutions, like religion, fatherland, family, culture—everything that people call the "pillars" of society.

PONIATOWSKA: But you belong to this society, don't you? You've been brought up and educated according to its rules. You are a Catholic.

BUÑUEL: On this score, I can speak only of what matters to me. Luckily, even as a young man I was able to glimpse something that, on the spiritual and poetic plane, goes far beyond Christian morality. I'm not so presumptuous as to want to make the world over. I know that in this sense my experience is sterile, but it does help me to clarify my films somewhat. . . . I cannot be untrue to myself. My morality is—

PONIATOWSKA: The morality of Nazarín?

BUÑUEL: Nazarín is entirely compatible with my morality.

PONIATOWSKA: The Nazarín who fails? The Nazarín who can do nothing with the Church? The unfrocked Nazarín who strides through the fields followed by two hysterical women?

BUÑUEL: Yes, that Nazarín.

PONIATOWSKA: But why? Christ—

BUÑUEL: Christ was crucified after He was found guilty. Wouldn't you call that a failure? Do you believe it is possible to be Christian in the *absolute* sense of the word?

PONIATOWSKA: Yes, by giving up everything, by withdrawing from the world.

BUÑUEL: No, no! I'm speaking of the *world,* of this earth on which we live. If Christ were to return, they'd crucify Him again. It is possible to be *relatively* Christian, but the *absolutely* pure, the *absolutely* innocent man—he's bound to fail. He's licked before he starts. I am sure that if Christ came back, the Church, the powerful churchmen, would condemn him again.

PONIATOWSKA: As a film, *Nazarín* seems to me strange and ambiguous.

BUÑUEL: You say ambiguous. I agree. The style is ambiguous and that's why it interests me. If a work is obvious, as far as I'm concerned it's finished. As for the religious problem, I'm convinced that the Christian in the pure and absolute meaning of the word has no place on this earth.

PONIATOWSKA: But why not?

BUÑUEL: Because in a world so badly made, as ours is, there is only one road—rebellion.

PONIATOWSKA: It's always the rebels who interest you? The doubters? People who are looking for something?

BUÑUEL: Mystery interests me. Mystery is the essential element in every work of art. I will never grow tired of repeating this.

PONIATOWSKA: What, according to you, is necessary to make a good film?

BUÑUEL: A good film must have the ambivalence of two opposed and related things. That's why I would so love to direct Juan Rulfo's *Pedro Paramo.* What appeals to me in Rulfo's work is the passage from mystery to reality. There is scarcely any transition, and this combination of reality and fantasy I like—I like it very much, but I don't know how to transfer it to a film.

PONIATOWSKA: Speaking of reality, you've never gone in for neorealism?

BUÑUEL: I think the only two good films neorealism has produced are *Umberto D* and *The Bicycle Thief.*

PONIATOWSKA: Zavattini?

BUÑUEL: As I've said before, Zavattini has raised completely banal actions to the level of the dramatic. Otherwise, neorealism doesn't interest me.

PONIATOWSKA: Because reality is described too faithfully?

BUÑUEL: Because reality is multiple, and for different people it can have a hundred different meanings. I want to have a total vision of reality, to enter the marvelous world of the unknown. All the rest lies within our reach every day of our lives.

With Yvonne Baby

[*Le Monde,* June 1, 1961]

BUÑUEL: I was not trying to be blasphemous, but then Pope John knows more about blasphemy than I. It was chance that led me to project the impious. If I had any pious ideas, perhaps I would express them, too. At sixty-one you don't indulge in childish behavior, and since I have no *parti pris,* I refuse to mix in the scandal. *Viridiana* follows a tradition, a line that has been mine ever since *L'Age d'Or;* they are thirty years apart, and I can say that these are the two films which I directed with the greatest freedom. It's been my experience to succeed sometimes more and sometimes less with my films, and also to make routine films in order to earn a living. However, I have always refused to make concessions, I've defended the principles I believe in. I went to Spain because that's my country and because I could work there with complete freedom.

BABY: Where did the idea for *Viridiana* come from?

BUÑUEL: Viridiana is a little-known saint from the time of St. Francis of Assisi, and I was struck by the name a long time ago. I thought of the story for the film while I was in Mexico; it came from a mental image. I always set about it this way, and then the work gushes forth like a fountain.

BABY: What was the image?

BUÑUEL: A young woman drugged by an old man. She is at the

mercy, then, of someone who, in other circumstances, could never have held her in his arms. I thought that the woman had to be pure, and I made her a novice. The idea of the beggars came later, because it seemed natural to me that a former nun would give them shelter on her property. Then I said to myself that I would love to see those beggars eating in the dining room of the manor house, sitting around the big table with the embroidered cloth and the candles. Suddenly I realized that they were grouping themselves into a painting, and da Vinci's "Last Supper" flashed into my mind. Finally, I associated the Hallelujah Chorus from Handel's *Messiah* with the beggars' orgy and dance, which are more striking if underlined in this way rather than by rock 'n' roll. I liked that effect. In the same way, I wanted to combine the Mozart Requiem and the love scene between the old man and the young woman, and to contrast the quiet Angelus prayer with the labor of the workers.

BABY: Which scenes or images have been especially criticized?

BUÑUEL: The burning crown of thorns, although burning is not profanation. And I've been criticized for showing a knife shaped like a cross. Such knives are found everywhere in Spain; I've seen a lot of them in Albacete. One day my sister, who is very religious, met a nun who was using one of these same little knives to peel apples. It is the photography that brings out the mischievous, surrealist nature of an object that is mass produced in all innocence.

Also, I am reproached for being cruel. But where is there any cruelty in the film? The novice gives proof of her humanity. The old man, admittedly a complex personality, is capable of kindness toward human beings and even toward a mere bee. His son wins our sympathy, more or less, and the beggars—of a classic type found in Spain—can be gross without being cruel. It is only the blind man who is mistrustful, hypocritical, and evil, like everyone afflicted with such an infirmity. That is why my blind people always have their moments of spitefulness.

In an early version of the film I envisaged the old man's son as a dwarf. But then I realized that people would say "How like Buñuel," and I gave up the idea. I try as much as I can to avoid my own commonplaces.

Essentially, I wanted to make a humorous film—corrosive humor, no doubt, but spontaneous—and one in which I express the erotic and religious obsessions of childhood. I belong to a devoutly Catholic family, and I was brought up by the Jesuits from the time I was eight until I was fifteen. A religious education and surrealism have left indelible traces upon my life. But I insist that I have never tried to prove anything and that I do not use the cinema as a pulpit from which to preach.

With George Sadoul

[*Les Lettres Françaises,* June 1, 1961]

BUÑUEL: When I make a film it is because I want and need to make it, and not at all because I want to create a sensation. This was true as early as 1928, with *Un Chien Andalou.* As for *Viridiana,* what is it that people take exception to? Throughout the film I stayed within the limits of the acceptable statement. My heroine is more virginal at the end than she was in the beginning. . . .

Some fools have also written that I made a "smutty" film. Down with smutty films! I hate them! [Buñuel shouted this, as if he were barking a military command.]

. . . Our world being what it is, I do not make my films for the public—by which I mean the quote public unquote. If this "public" is conventional, bound and perverted by tradition, that is not its fault but the fault of society. It is very difficult, very rare, to be able to make a film that pleases both this public and your friends, the people whose judgment matters to you. . . .

I am very much attached to Nazarín. He is a priest. He could as easily be a hairdresser or a waiter. What interests me about him is that he stands by his ideas, that these ideas are inacceptable to society at large, and that after his adventures with prostitutes, thieves, and so forth, they lead him to being irrevocably damned by the prevailing social order. . . .

With Kenji Kanesaka

[*Film Culture*, Spring 1962]

The young Japanese film critic Kenji Kanesaka visited Luis Buñuel at his home in Mexico City where he recorded the following interview:

KANESAKA: Congratulations on your success with *Viridiana*. I caught up with *The Young One* last night.

BUÑUEL: I would like you to see *Viridiana*.

KANESAKA: In Japan, unfortunately, we could only see two of your films, *Un Chien Andalou* and *Los Olvidados*. But even so, I know that movie people with progressive ideas value your achievements very highly. You have made over twenty pictures. Which among them do you most recommend us to see. *El* and *Robinson Crusoe?*

BUÑUEL: *El* and *Nazarín*. About *Robinson Crusoe* I am not so sure. Also you may not find a proper print. Among others, when one makes twenty-one or twenty-two pictures, there are some that are not at all good.

KANESAKA: *Un Chien Andalou* came to Japan very recently for the first time. Every book says that you and Salvador Dali wrote the script together and you directed it. Can you say which particular ideas were yours and which were Dali's? Would you say you were influenced by Dali? Do you have anything to say about Dali since?

BUÑUEL: It is true—that story was written by both of us. I was director, producer and owner. But now I'm not so sure because it seems that everybody has rights to the film. The film was made thirty-two years ago and I do not remember much about the details regarding our collaboration. What I know about Dali and me is that now we belong to a totally different world. For Dali has gone to a world of men who make money.

KANESAKA: I think the dream sequence in *Los Olvidados,* for instance, is more genuinely surrealistic than surrealism. Some hold a view that you synthesize different approaches of the documentary and *avant-garde* cinema.

BUÑUEL: I always try to be free of *avant-garde* affectations. On the other hand, although I had observed the situations of the slums for eighteen months before shooting *Los Olvidados,* I would hesitate to call it a documentary film, as I have reflected my own ideas in the film. There is not much sense in attaching labels. In essence, we make films the way we please and some can make good ones. Some cannot.

KANESAKA: I think your style is imitated a great deal by young directors. Especially your images of "violence."

BUÑUEL: If I employ "violence" it is not violence for its own sake. It is to express something else—perhaps something in the world of ideas. In this sense there has been no real influence of me on the world of films. But of course I do not see many films lately unless they are strongly recommended by my friends.

KANESAKA: Have you seen any *Nouvelle Vague* films?

BUÑUEL: I saw *Hiroshima, Mon Amour* and *400 Blows.* I like them.

KANESAKA: Do you think these two are much different from each other? Will they both remain in the history of film art like *Los Olvidados* does?

BUÑUEL: They are quite different from each other. *400 Blows* is something like the vogue. It pursues the momentary, private truth, while *Hiroshima, Mon Amour* intends to deal with a universal problem. Perhaps the latter has a better chance to remain in the film repertory. I think I heard that Resnais said he liked my work.

KANESAKA: Is the intention to study people's inner problems in order to finally reach social and universal problems the one that most corresponds between your work and Resnais?

BUÑUEL: It may be so. But I think in my own terms. *Hiroshima, Mon Amour* has a bad narration. It has old-fashioned music. And the last part—where the man and the woman are finding it hard to break away from each other—is endlessly repetitious. But still

I value the first three reels very highly. I may say they convey the anguish of our time. But essentially this feeling is unexplainable. Something like an aura that surrounds the film.

KANESAKA: How about Japanese films? Do you find Kurosawa interesting?

BUÑUEL: I only saw *Rashomon* and *Gate of Hell*. I like them in a different way from *Hiroshima, Mon Amour*. I like Resnais' film from the viewpoint of ideas and politics, and the Japanese films from that of lyricism and exoticism.

KANESAKA: By lyricism do you mean visual beauty? Have you seen *Ikiru*?

BUÑUEL: I have not seen enough Japanese films to pass any judgment. Oh, yes, I saw *Seven Samurai* too. Kurosawa is superficial but an extraordinary master of spectacle. I like his films very much. *Gate of Hell* contains something more universal in that it has love as a central theme. I was a member of the jury at the Cannes Film Festival the year it won the prize. I might have missed it if I hadn't been. But anyway, the Japanese films I saw are a lot better than Hollywood films today. . . .

KANESAKA: I have just made a survey of Hollywood and the independent film making in America, and I think that the film making in America is coming into a new era. What advice would you give to the young film maker? Should he concentrate on expressing himself or on pleasing the audience?

BUÑUEL: There have always been two kinds of cinema, the "commercial" and the "artistic." There are always some men who will try to express their inner world, to convey it to others through the medium of the film, which is above all a marvelous tool for artistic creation. At the same time, films are made to please the culturally inferior masses, who are so either for social or economic reasons. Thus such films are apt to be superficial, stereotyped, easy to understand, and they usually kowtow to the morals and politics of the different governments. This could be a good definition of the commercial film. Sometimes, very seldom, a creative film is also commercial but then this quality of commerciality is the predicate whereas the subject is art.

3. BUÑUEL'S WORKS

SURREALIST TEXTS

ON LOVE

[*La Révolution Surréaliste*, No. 12, December 15, 1929]

What sort of hope do you place in love?

L. B.: If I love, all my hope. If I don't love, none.

How do you envisage the transition from the idea of love to the fact of loving? Would you sacrifice your freedom, willingly or not, to love? Have you ever done so? Would you, if need be, sacrifice a cause you had believed you must defend in order not to fall short of your duty to love? Would you consent to not being what you could have become, if that were the price of your being sure of love? What would you think of a man who would go so far as to betray his conviction to please the woman he loves? Can such proof of love be asked or obtained?

L. B.: Point 1—For me, only the fact of loving exists. Point 2—I would willingly sacrifice my freedom to love. I have already done so. Point 3—I would sacrifice a cause I believed in to love, but that kind of decision must be made on the spur of the moment. Point 4—Yes. Point 5—I would think well of him. However, in spite of that, I would ask the man not to betray his convictions. I would go so far as to insist that he not.

Would you consider that you had the right to deprive yourself temporarily of the presence of the person you love, because you know how absence stimulates love—although at the same time you acknowledge the fact that such calculated behavior is unworthy?

L. B.: I would not want to be separated from the person I love. Not at any price.

Do you believe that a great love can triumph over sordid conditions of life, or does a sordid life defeat even a great love?

L. B.: I don't know.

A GIRAFFE

[*Surréalisme au Service de la Révolution*, No. 6, May 15, 1933]

This giraffe, life-size, is a simple piece of wood cut out in the form of a giraffe, but, in contrast to other wooden animals of the same kind, this one has a distinguishing difference. Each spot on her skin—which does not look in any way unusual from ten or fifteen feet away—is made of one of several things: a little lid that the viewer can easily open by turning it on an invisible hinge installed on one side; or an object of whatever sort; or a hole that lets the daylight through (the giraffe is only about an inch thick); or a small cavity containing the various objects enumerated below.

Note that the meaning of this giraffe is not really expressed until she is completed; that is, until each of her spots fulfills the function intended for it. This is a costly procedure but nonetheless possible.

Everything Is Entirely Realizable

In order to hide the objects that must be found behind the giraffe, it must be placed in front of a black wall thirty feet high and forty feet long. The surface of the wall must be perfectly smooth. At the foot of this wall there must be a bed of asphodels, its dimensions to be the same as those of the wall.

What Must Be Found in Each Giraffe Spot

In the first: The core of the spot is a little mechanism that is quite complicated and resembles the movement of a watch. Centered in the serrated wheels of the works, a little propeller whirls madly. A faint smell of decay emanates from the whole. Upon leaving the

spot, pick up an album lying on the ground at the giraffe's feet. Sit down in a corner of the garden and leaf through the album, which contains dozens of photographs of wretched and deserted little squares. They are squares in old Castilian towns: Alba de Tormes, Soria, Madrigal de las Altas Torres, Orgaz, Burgo de Osma, Tordesillas, Simancas, Siguenza, Cadalso de los Vidrios and, above all, Toledo.

In the second: If it is opened at noon, as the instructions on the outside indicate, one finds oneself confronting the eye of a cow set in its socket, complete with lashes and lid. The spectator's image is reflected in the eye. The lid closes suddenly, ending the self-contemplation.

In the third: On opening this spot, one finds these two words against a background of red velvet: Américo Castro.* Since the letters are detachable, one can make all sorts of combinations with them.

In the fourth: There is a little grating, like that of a prison. Through the grating, one can hear a full-fledged orchestra of a hundred musicians playing the overture to *Die Meistersinger*.

In the fifth: Two billiard balls fall out with a crash as soon as this spot is opened. Inside, nothing is left standing but a parchment rolled up and tied with a string. Unroll it and read this poem:

To Richard the Lion-Hearted

From the choirs to the cellar, from the cellar to the hill, from the hill to hell, to the sabbath agonies of winter.

From the choir to the sex of the she-wolf who fled into the timeless forests of the Middle Ages.

Verba vedata sunt fodido en culo et puto gafo, it was the taboo sign of the first hut built in the endless woods, it was the taboo sign of the dejection of the she-goat, from which issued the masses of people who built the cathedrals.

Blasphemies floated over the swamps, the people trembled under the whips of the bishops of broken marble, the female parts were used to shape toads.

* Professor at the University of Madrid, ex-ambassador to Berlin.

With time, the nuns turned green again, from their dry sides green branches bloomed, the incubi gave them the eye while the soldiers pissed on the convent walls, and the centuries wallowed in the lepers' sores.

Clusters of dry nuns hung from the windows, making a sweet sound of orisons thanks to the warm spring wind.

I'll have to pay my tithe, Richard the Lion-Hearted, *fodido en puto gafo.*

In the sixth: The spot moves from one side of the giraffe to the other. You can see the landscape through the hole; some thirty feet away, my mother—Mme Buñuel—dressed like a laundress, kneels by a little stream and washes clothes. There are a few cows behind her.

In the seventh: An old sack, daubed with plaster.

In the eighth: This spot is slightly concave and is covered with very fine, curly blond hairs taken from the pubes of a young Danish adolescent with light-blue eyes, a plump body, skin bronzed by the sun, all innocence and candor. The viewer must blow softly on the hair.

In the ninth: In place of the spot one finds a large, dark night moth with a death's head between its wings.

In the tenth: Inside the spot one finds a largish quantity of bread dough. The viewer is tempted to knead it with his fingers. Well-concealed razor blades will bloody his hands.

In the eleventh: A pig's bladder takes the place of the spot. Nothing else. Take up the giraffe and transport her to Spain and place her at Masada del Vicario, four and one half miles from Calanda, south of the Aragon River, with her head pointing north. Burst the bladder with your fist and look through the hole. A poor, whitewashed cottage will be seen in the midst of a desertlike landscape. A fig tree is a few yards from the door, to the fore. In the background, mountains that look as if they have been peeled, and olive trees. An old peasant may, at this moment, come out of the house, barefoot.

In the twelfth: A very fine photograph of Christ's head crowned with thorns, but roaring with laughter.

In the thirteenth: At the back of the spot, a very beautiful rose, larger than life and made of apple parings. The androecia consist of bloody meat. A few hours later, the rose will turn black. The next day, it will putrify. Three days later, a legion of worms will crawl over it.

In the fourteenth: A black hole. One hears this dialogue, whispered in great anguish:

WOMAN'S VOICE: No, I beg of you. Don't freeze.
MAN'S VOICE: Yes, I must. I could not look you in the face. (*A sound of rain is heard.*)
WOMAN'S VOICE: I love you just the same, I'll always love you, but don't freeze. *Do . . . not . . . freeze.* (*Pause*)
MAN'S VOICE (*Very low, very gentle*): My little corpse . . . (*Pause. Sound of stifled laughter*)

A bright light flashes on suddenly inside the spot. In this light, a few hens can be seen pecking.

In the fifteenth: A tiny double casement window, an exact replica in miniature of a normal-sized window. All of a sudden, a puff of dense white smoke issues from it, followed a few seconds later by a distant explosion. (Smoke and explosion must be like those of cannon, seen and heard from a mile or so away.)

In the sixteenth: On opening the spot, one sees an Annunciation of Fra Angelico, very well framed and lighted but in pitiable condition: slashed with a knife, dripping resin, the Virgin's face carefully bedaubed with excrement, the eyes pierced by needles, the sky marked by the inscription in large letters: DOWN WITH THE MOTHER OF THE TURK.

In the seventeenth: A powerful jet of live steam will belch forth from the spot as soon as it is opened, hideously blinding the spectator.

In the eighteenth: Opening this spot causes the following objects to fall with excruciating effect: needles, thread, a thimble, pieces of cloth, two empty matchboxes, a stub of candle, a very old pack of cards, a few buttons, empty perfume bottles, smelling salts, a square watch, a door knob, a broken pipe, two letters,

foot braces, and a few live spiders. Everything scatters in the most disturbing fashion. (This is the only spot that symbolizes death.)

In the nineteenth: Behind the spot a sketch less than a yard square represents the Sahara desert under blinding sunlight. All over the sand, hundreds of little waxen figurines of Marists, their white aprons standing out against their dark cassocks. In the heat, the Marists melt little by little. (There must be a reserve of several million of these Mary-worshipers on hand.)

In the twentieth: On opening this spot, we see twelve little terracotta busts of Mme ———* lined up on four planks. They are marvelously well made and look like her, despite their tiny dimensions. Through a magnifying glass, we note that the little teeth are made of ivory. All the teeth of the last bust have been pulled out.

LETTER TO PÉPIN

[This text was written in 1928 and addressed to José (or Pépin) Bello, a friend of Buñuel's at that time. It was found by J. F. Aranda and published in Positif, *in November 1959.]*

DEAR PÉPIN,

How moved I was to read your letter and to see how modestly you recall that unforgettable day of the 29th, when San Valero the Boastful passed with his vaulted window over our heads above the sidewalk of Cecilia Gasca! You have always been very good and you remembered that day of the 29th. I, instead, decided to have my heart examined on San Valero's day. I am not well. I lose strength every day. When the doctor started to examine me, a great windstorm arose outside; it was so violent that it pulled off all the little windows of the balcony as if they had been so many arms. The dust in the street was so thick that one could not even see the priests pass. A vast number of sewing machines, sticks, pots with funnels, and little islands of Formosa surrounded by banks of tuna whirled rapidly in the wind, coming forth to shine

* I cannot reveal her name.—L.B.

for an instant before being swallowed up once more in the unknown.

Neither the doctor nor my father could make anything of it. My good father remonstrated that this windstorm represented a serious danger in his life and that he could not tolerate such an indecent diagnosis even for an instant. The doctor said that while this was perhaps so, my forebear had always queened it over his pawn and that no matter what a veteran he might be, he, the doctor, spoke with greater authority and more briefly—another bone for another dog.

My father took me by the hand and led me out into the street. The wind's violence was at its height. What a smell of wax! A disgusting buzzing made us dizzy, and great powerful gusts prevented us from going forward. The tornado threw hundreds of half-naked priests at us, hurling them with such force that we were nearly knocked over. I noticed that all of them, as they banged us on the nose, started to sing the same song through their teeth. It went something like this:

> *Little girl, little girl, pretty little girl,*
> *You don't know what the sea, what the sea is;*
> *If you knew, my life, my dolly,*
> *You'd soon start to turn about quickly.*

Now the moral of the motet may seem frivolous, but it's enough to remind me of the days when I was a café waiter and a little before noon my father would bring my daily couscous to the café on an unforgettable gold platter which he would leave a mile or two from the tables.

The priests became more numerous as they struck us on the nose. The song was like an unintelligible buzzing, which is why I knew that in it there was an allusion of a scarcely respectable nature to my absent mother. But tell me, Pépin, who cares if the designs at the tops of the columns are of one style or another? Tell me. What the devil!

Well, finally the mustache of one of the priests got caught in the venerable white mustache of my father. The priest stayed

there, ready for any eventuality, as all good upstanding people are. To my great regret, he took advantage of the occasion to address the following lecture to me:

"I tell you truly, my son, San Valero never failed to respect the code. The art of his period—and I am speaking to you now without bitterness—consisted in keeping out noises, parasites of the great naves wherein alone the smoke of battles could rise. There [were] wandering bosoms, stone wings, sad furrows, joyous picnics on the tombstones, acts of incest, the words we hear only at night, and heaps of wood piled up by the hands of children.

"But San Valero, sitting facing the till, paid no attention. He was never short by so much as a penny. He, his father, and his grandfather were all accountants, and better than accountants— engineers. It's a pity that San Valero's son, who is also called San Valero, hasn't enough money to pay for his studies. But that's part of the next chapter."

At these last words, night fell. The priest was silent and began skillfully and lovingly to gather together his scattered flock. When they were all assembled, he started them on the steep descent that led to the valley.

Very Important

The descent led to a valley that I could not cross. Ten huge priests with powerful scimitars barred the way. On the shining blades of their curved sabers I could make out the following inscription: "The descent leads to a v . . ." The last word, partly effaced, was hard to interpret. Could it be "vale" or, perhaps, "wake"? Perhaps neither one nor the other. Or was it a photograph of the Last Supper, with the diners replaced by as many pyxes containing the Host, the pyx in Christ's place giving a smart rap to the one leaning its head on His shoulder, and the last pyx—the one standing for Judas—holding a dray in its hand.

I fell into a rage. Are you priests or idolaters? If you're the former, let's fight; if not, then may God pay you. But already the evening, the valley, the wake, the scimitars are no more than the tap-tap of a typewriter operated by the chief of the technocrats

himself. He takes the paper out of the machine, puts it in an envelope, and writes, by hand, the following address in pencil:

> M. Alcide Pantaleón
> Modest Knight, Pantico, S.A.
> Write me.

Write me.

Luis

Realistic details:

My sister recognizes that that particular San Valero's day was very strange in Saragossa: "You saw on San Pablo's Street [the street of prostitutes] people who were not usually there—baronesses, countesses, the de Parellada women wearing big hats! We had to go down some steps to enter San Pablo's church. Inside, on the altar to San Valero, who was a blackish saint, the figure stood with a finger raised, holding a tart such as one eats at a wake. Lastly, at home we ate a San Valero made of sugar, and everyone felt very happy and very sad. Perhaps because that was the day grandfather died."

FILMS

UN CHIEN ANDALOU (scenario)

NOTE: The version of this scenario published in *La Révolution Surréaliste* [No. 12, December 15, 1929] is the only one I authorize. It expresses without reservation of any kind my complete adherence to the thought and activity of the surrealists. *Un Chien Andalou* would not exist if surrealism had not existed.

"A successful film" is what the majority of people who saw it thought. But what can I do about people who are crazy for anything new, even if the novelty outrages their inmost convictions, or about a venal or insincere press, or about that pack of imbeciles who found beauty or poetry in what is, in essence, nothing less than a desperate, passionate appeal to murder.

—L.B.

PROLOGUE

Once upon a time . . .

A balcony at night. A man is sharpening a razor near the balcony. The man looks through the window at the sky and sees . . .

A small cloud advancing toward the moon, which is at the full.

Then the head of a young girl, her eyes open wide. The razor blade advances toward one of the eyes.

The small cloud passes in front of the moon.

The razor blade passes over the young girl's eyeball, sectioning it.

END OF PROLOGUE

Eight years later.

A deserted street. It is raining.

A man, dressed in a dark-gray suit, appears on a bicycle.

He wears a sort of maid's cap, a ruffled cape, and a peplum of white linen over an ordinary suit.

A rectangular box, diagonally striped in black and white, is attached to his chest by leather thongs. The man pedals mechanically, not touching the handlebars, his hands resting on his knees.

Torso shot of the man, seen from behind down to the thighs, and superimposed on it a lengthwise shot of the street down which he is making his way with his back to the camera.

The man comes toward the camera until the striped box is in close-up.

An ordinary room on the third floor of a building on the same street. In the center, a young girl is seated, dressed in lively colors. She is reading a book attentively. Suddenly she shudders, listens curiously, and throws her book on a nearby sofa. The book stays open. On one of the pages is seen a reproduction of Vermeer's "The Lacemakers." The young girl is convinced that something is going on; she gets up, turns halfway from the camera, and walks rapidly to the window.

The man we have seen earlier has just stopped downstairs in the street. Out of inertia, without showing the least resistance, he falls in the gutter with his bicycle into a mud puddle.

The young girl makes a gesture of rage, of resentment, and rushes toward the stairs to go down to the street.

Close-up of the man stretched on the ground, in the identical position in which he fell; his face is without expression.

The young girl comes out of the house and rushes toward the cyclist; she kisses his mouth, eyes, nose, frantically.

The rain increases to the point of making the foregoing scene disappear.

Fade-in to the box, whose oblique lines are superimposed on those of the rain. Hands holding a little key open the box, from which they take a necktie wrapped in tissue paper. The rain, the box, the tissue paper, and the tie must all be marked by oblique lines which vary only in width.

The same room.

The young girl is standing beside the bed, contemplating the accessories the man had been wearing—the linen cap, cape, and

peplum, the box, stiff collar, a dark, one-toned tie—everything laid out as if these objects were being worn by someone stretched out on the bed. The young girl finally decides to pick up the stiff collar, from which she removes the monochrome tie, and replaces it with the striped tie, which she has just taken from the box. She replaces it in the same spot, and then sits down beside the bed in the pose of someone keeping watch at a wake. (Note: The bed —that is to say, the coverlet and the pillow—is slightly mussed and dented, as if a human body were really resting on it.)

The young woman has the feeling that someone is behind her and turns to see who it is. Without the least surprise, she sees the man, this time without any of his accessories, looking very attentively at something in his right hand. In this great attentiveness there is an element of severe anxiety.

The woman draws near him and looks in her turn into his hand.

Close-up of the hand, in the center of which a cluster of ants swarms from a black hole. None of the ants falls.

Fade to the underarm hair of a young girl stretched on the sand on a sunny beach. Fade to a sea urchin whose mobile spines wave slightly. Fade to the head of another young woman (taken in an abrupt plunging shot), enclosed in an iris. The iris opens to reveal the fact that this girl is in the middle of a group of people who are trying to force their way through a street barricade set up by the police.

In the center of the circle, the young woman is trying to pick up with a stick a severed hand with painted nails that is lying on the ground. One of the policemen comes up to her and roundly scolds her; then he stoops and picks up the hand, which he carefully wraps and places in the box the cyclist had been carrying. He gives the whole thing to the young girl and salutes in smart military fashion when she thanks him.

At the moment the policeman hands her the box, the young woman is overcome by an extraordinary emotion that sets her completely apart from everything. She is as if bemused by the echoes of far-off, religious music—music that perhaps she has heard in her earliest childhood.

The crowd, whose curiosity is now satisfied, begins to scatter in all directions.

This scene will have been observed by the people we left in the third-floor room. We see them through the balcony windowpanes whence they could observe the scene described above. When the policeman hands the young girl the box, the two balcony characters seem likewise overcome by the same emotion as she, an emotion that reduces them to tears. Their heads nod as if they are following the rhythm of the same impalpable music.

The man looks at the young woman, making a gesture as if to say: "Did you see that? Didn't I tell you?"

She looks once more into the street and at the young girl who seems now glued to the spot, in a state of absolute inhibition. Cars pass by at extravagant speeds. Suddenly one of them passes over her, mutilating her horribly.

Then, with the decisiveness of someone who has a full right to do so, the man approaches the young woman and, after looking lasciviously into her eyes, seizes her breasts. Close-up of the hungry hands on the breasts. Her breasts appear from beneath the dress. Then we see an expression of terrible, almost mortal, anguish appear on the man's face. A trickle of bloody saliva runs from his mouth onto the exposed breast of the young woman.

The breasts disappear to be replaced by thighs which the man continues to palp. His facial expression has changed. His eyes are bright with meanness and excitement. His mouth, at first wide open, shuts tight as if drawn in by a sphincter.

The young woman withdraws toward the back of the room, followed by the man in the same attitude.

Suddenly, she makes a decisive gesture that separates his arms, thus freeing her of his aggressive contact.

The man's mouth contracts in rage.

She is aware that a disagreeable or violent scene is about to take place.

She withdraws step by step into a corner where she protects herself behind a little table.

He takes on the attitude of the villain in a melodrama; he looks

about everywhere, searching for something. At his feet, he sees the end of a rope and picks it up with his right hand. His left hand searches the floor and grabs an identical piece of rope.

The young woman, flattened against the wall, follows the actions of her attacker with terror.

He advances on her, hauling with great difficulty whatever is attached to the two ropes.

We see first a cork, then a melon, then two brothers of a teaching order, and finally two magnificent grand pianos. The pianos are filled with the carcasses of two donkeys whose hoofs, tails, croups, and excrements overflow the body of the instrument. When one of the pianos passes before the camera, we see a great donkey's head leaning against the keyboard.

The man, dragging this weight with great effort, is straining desperately toward the young woman. He knocks over chairs, tables, a standing lamp, and so on. The asses' croups become entangled with everything. The lamp suspended from the ceiling swings back and forth until the end of the scene.

Just as the man is about to reach the young woman, she bounds away and eludes him. Her attacker, dropping the ropes, rushes after her. The young woman opens a door through which she disappears into the next room, but not rapidly enough to close it. The hand of the man manages to pass through the opening and it remains there, caught at the wrist.

From the adjoining room, the young woman, pulling the door even tighter, looks at the hand that clenches painfully and more and more slowly. The ants reappear and now spread over the door. Immediately she turns her head toward the interior of the second room, identical with the first, but rendered different in appearance by the lighting. The young woman sees . . .

The same bed. The man, whose hand is still caught in the door, is stretched out on it. This time he is dressed in his linen accessories, and has the box on his chest. He makes not the slightest gesture; his eyes are wide open and have an ominous expression, as if to say: "At this moment something really extraordinary is about to happen!"

Toward three o'clock in the morning.

On the landing near the entrance to the flat, a new character—seen from behind—has just paused. He presses the bell of the apartment door behind which the foregoing events have taken place. One sees neither the bell nor its electric hammer, but through two holes above the door where the bell would be can be seen two hands moving a silver cocktail shaker. Their movement is instantaneous, as in ordinary films when one presses on an electric bell.

The man in the bed trembles.

The young woman goes to open the door.

The new character goes directly to the bed and firmly orders the man to get up. He obeys, but so unwillingly that the other brutally forces him to rise.

After ripping off the man's linen cap, cape, and peplum, the attacker throws them out the window one by one. The box follows, then the straps, which the man has tried in vain to conceal. This attempt causes the new arrival to punish the first man by sending him to stand against one of the walls of the room.

All the attacker's movements are executed with his back to the camera. He turns around now, for the first time, to get something on the other side of the room.

At that moment, the focus blurs. The new arrival walks in slow motion and we see that his features are identical to those of the first man; they are one and the same person; only the later arrival looks younger and more attractive, as the first man must have looked some years before.

The new character goes toward the back of the room, preceded by the camera, which he follows; he is visible to the waist only.

A desk, toward which our individual moves, now comes into view. Two books are on the desk, along with other schoolboy accouterments. Their position and moral sense will be determined with care.

He takes the two books and turns around to join the first male character. At that moment, everything returns to normal—that is, the fuzzy focus clears and the slow motion ceases.

When he has drawn near the first man, he orders him to raise his arms in the position of the cross, places a book in each hand, and orders him to stay this way as punishment.

The man being punished now assumes an expression full of shrewdness and treachery. He turns on the new arrival. The books, which he continues to hold, turn into revolvers.

The later arrival looks at him with a tenderness that grows visibly, moment by moment.

The character who had worn the linen accessories, threatening the other with his revolvers, forces him into a "Hands up!" position and, despite his obeying, fires both arms at him. In a half-body shot, the latter arrival falls, mortally wounded, his features contracted in pain. The soft focus has returned and the fall forward is in even slower motion than the sequence before.)

From a distance, we see the wounded man fall, only this time he is not in the room but in a grove. At his side, we see a woman sitting, motionless, and photographed from behind. Her back is bare and she is leaning forward slightly.

As he falls, the wounded man clutches at her back. One of his trembling hands is turned toward himself, the other touches the skin of her naked shoulders. Finally he falls to the ground.

Long-distance shot. A few passers-by and park guards rush to give him aid. They raise his body in their arms and bear him off through a woods.

Enter the passionate limping man.

And we return to the same room. The door in which the hand had been imprisoned opens slowly. The young woman we know appears. She closes the door behind her and looks attentively at the wall against which the assassin had stood.

The man is no longer there. The wall in intact, without a single piece of furniture or ornament.

The young woman makes a gesture of impatience and irritation.

Once more we see the wall, in the middle of which is a small black spot.

This little spot seen from closer range turns out to be a death's-head moth. The moth in close-up.

The death's-head pattern of the moth's wings fills the screen.

In a half-body shot, the man with the linen accessories is shown putting his hand quickly to his mouth, like a man who is losing his teeth. The young woman looks at him scornfully.

When the man withdraws his hand, we see that his mouth has disappeared. The young woman seems to say: "Well, what next?" and tidies up her lipline with her lipstick.

We see the head of the man again and, at the spot where his mouth was, hairs are beginning to grow.

The young woman stifles a cry on seeing this and quickly glances at her armpit; it is completely clean-shaven. Disdainfully she sticks out her tongue at him, throws a shawl over her shoulders, and, opening the connecting door beside her, she passes into the adjacent room, which is a big beach.

Near the water a third male character waits. The two greet each other very amicably and walk together, following the curve of the waves.

Shot of their legs and the waves lapping at their feet.

The camera follows them on a dolly. The waves gently toss at their feet first the linen cap, cape, and peplum, then the striped box, then the white bands, and finally the bicycle. This shot holds a moment longer as the sea tosses up nothing at all.

They continue their walk along the beach, fading little by little, as the following words appear in the sky:

IN SPRING

Everything has changed. Now we see a desert without horizon. Planted in the center, buried in sand up to their chests, are the principal male character and the young woman, both blind, their clothing torn, devoured by the sun's rays and by a swarm of insects.

L'AGE D'OR (synopsis)

Some scorpions live among the rocks. Clambering up one of these, a bandit spies a group of archbishops seated, singing, in the midst

of a rocky landscape. The bandit runs to tell his friends about the presence of the people from Majorca (the archbishops) nearby. When he reaches his hut, he finds his friends in a strange state of weakness and depression. They take up their arms and go out, all except the youngest, who can no longer even get up. They start off walking among the rocks but their strength fails them, and one by one they fall by the wayside. The bandit chieftain slumps down in despair. From where he is sitting, he hears the sound of the sea and perceives the people from Majorca, who have now been reduced to skeletons scattered among the stones.

An enormous naval caravan lands on the coast at this rugged and desolate spot. The caravan is made up of priests, soldiers, nuns, ministers, and various people in civilian dress. They head for the place where the skeletons of the Majorcans lie. Following the example of the authorities who lead the funeral procession, the rest of the people take off their hats.

They are founding Imperial Rome. The first stone is being laid when piercing cries distract everyone's attention. A few feet away, a man and woman are struggling in a passionate embrace. They are separated. The man is beaten and policemen lead him away.

The man and woman will be the protagonists of this film. Thanks to a document that reveals the man's high position and the important humanitarian and patriotic mission entrusted to him by the government, he is soon freed. From this moment on, he is completely absorbed by love. During a scene of unconsummated love-making, the tension of which is created by the violence of uncommitted acts, the protagonist is called to the telephone by the high functionary who has entrusted him with the humanitarian mission in question. The minister upbraids him. Because he has neglected his task, thousands of old people and innocent children have perished. The protagonist of the film greets this accusation with curses, and, not bothering to listen further, he returns to the woman he loves at the very moment when an inexplicable stroke of fate intervenes to separate them even more definitively. Subsequently we see him throw a burning pine tree out the window, then a huge harvesting machine, then an archbishop, followed by a giraffe and some feathers. All this comes hurtling down at the

moment the survivors of the Château de Selligny cross the snow-covered drawbridge. The Duc de Blangis is clearly Jesus Christ. This last episode is accompanied by a *paso doble.*°

L'AGE D'OR (excerpts from shooting script)

61. General view of the Vatican, taken from the air, if possible. Sustained view of the Vatican.

The ancient mistress of the pagan world has for some centuries now been the secular seat of the Church. A few aspects of the Vatican, the strongest pillar of the Church.

62. Principal façade of the Vatican, taken from a distance. Rapid dissolve.
Pan in on a section of this façade. Among other architectural elements, we notice a window.
Rapid dissolve to a focus on the window.
We see a piece of paper—in fact, a letter—patched to one of the squares to replace a piece of broken glass.
Rapid dissolve to a close-up of the letter.
63. The letter fills the entire camera screen, so that one can easily read what is written on it. The text of the letter follows:

I've already spoken to the director, who will set bail very low. If you wish, we can go directly to the man at the station, so that you can leave the chauffeur for Pierrot and Antonia. I am very eager to know what you were referring to in your telegram. Nothing more to say. Until we meet. An embrace from your

Primo.

64. View of a street that could as well be a street in Rome as in any other modern city.
Sustained shot of this view.

° In this film, we see along with other details, a blind man being mistreated, a dog being crushed, a boy almost gratuitously killed by his father, an old woman being slapped.—A.K.

But the ancient Imperial City has also entered the whirlpool of modern life.

65. Near view of a mass of cars at a traffic intersection.

66. A terrace café on a street crowded with people.

Rapid dissolve to a partial view of the terrace. Four or five tables with clients. At one of them, a woman sits sobbing, her hair in disorder, her face in her hands. No one pays any attention to her.

Different picturesque views of the Great City:

67. An utterly undistinguished shop front.

67a. Undistinguished fountain with spout.

67b. Fragment of wall.

68. Entrance to an even more commonplace building.

69. A sidewalk along which a few pedestrians are passing. One is literally covered with dust. He shakes it off his lapels, but very delicately, as if the lapels were the only dusty part of his clothing.

70. Another sidewalk. Among other people, a very respectable-looking gentleman passes by, kicking a violin that has been dropped on the ground. He does this with the expression of dissimulation that people put on when, for example, they don't want to be observed trying not to walk on the cracks in a sidewalk.

71. A near view of the legs of the passers-by, so that we can see the violin being kicked forward by the same gentleman. Follow him a moment with the dolly.

72. A deserted avenue that recalls Versailles. Leafy. In the foreground, there is a statue on the left which balances a stone on its head. We see a man (73) coming toward the camera from that same direction, also balancing a stone on his head. He disappears under the camera, since this sequence will have been shot from above.

73. Close-up of the man, seen to the waist, advancing with the stone balanced on his hat. He is an elderly man and wears a beard and mustache.

74. Background of indiscriminately chosen façades, palings, walls, and so on. Traveling shot. Policemen and a suspect enter the scene. They pass a stocking ad, which the suspect follows with

his eyes as the group comes forward, so that he is obliged to turn his head. The dolly stops when they turn a corner.

75. The ad shows a woman's legs clad in sheer silk stockings, and spread wide, like those of a seated woman who spreads her legs. The ad is caught first in close-up and then the camera moves back.

76. Rapid dissolve to another background of façades with another ad. The suspect enters the camera's range with the policemen; passing the ad, he stops all of a sudden, as if powerfully attracted by whatever the poster represents. The guards stop, too, unable to mask their surprise, but this reaction is very brief, and as soon as they recover themselves they hustle their prisoner along (77). Brutally, and striking him for good measure, they drag their prisoner away from this vision.

77. Insert of the prisoner against the previous sequence. His eyes are still devouring the ad (78). The efforts of the police to make him follow them finally shake him from his absorption. Reconnect with 76.

78. Close-up of the ad. It advertises the excellence of a certain hand cream. A woman's hand, very white, is shown with the ring finger extended and inserted into a hole painted on the poster. Rapid dissolve to a live hand, very similar to the one on the ad. It is oscillating rapidly and pressing on the finger that disappears in the hole. The effect of this nervous movement will be extremely disturbing, since its significance is clearly masturbatory.

79. Sidewalk or fence taken in a lengthwise shot. From a fair distance away, we see the policemen and the suspect approaching. When they reach the foreground, one of the policemen, with a rapid gesture, brings the others to a halt. We see that he is about to take a cigarette from his vest pocket (80). He lights it, and, taking one arm of the suspect while his companion takes the other, they go on their way, leaving the scene by moving out of range to the left.

80. Filmed from behind, the group has the suspect in the center. Reconnect with previous shot of the policeman lighting a cigarette. The suspect turns his head toward the camera. His attention has been caught by a third ad we will already have seen on the wall.

This time his expression is more full of desire, lasciviousness, and love than before (81). One of the guards rouses him from his contemplation of the ad so that he will go along with them. Tie in gestures with previous sequence.

81. An ad with the picture of a woman's head voluptuously thrown back. She greatly resembles the suspect's mistress. The announcement may very well have to do with a great star and one of her films. Rapid dissolve to the real head of the young girl, in a pose similar to that of the actress on the poster. (At this moment, insert in montage the head of the suspect in the background. His expression will be full of love and desire.) The camera moves back a few yards on its dolly and we see the young girl in the throes of a kind of passionate frenzy, stretched out, trembling, on the grass in some garden. This boom shot will be so taken as to give a coincidental reality to the image the suspect has of her (he substitutes the head in the ad for that of his mistress) and to reveal what, in fact, the young girl was feeling or doing at the moment the suspect was looking at her. Dissolve to the ad, caught from the same angle as before the earlier dissolve.

82. The suspect and the policemen move away, blocking the camera eye, and walk down the street.

83. Close-up of the young girl, whose voluptuous lassitude leaves no doubt as to what was meant by the preceding shots of her. She pulls herself together slowly and lazily. At last on her feet, she moves off, the camera following her from a distance. She walks toward the main entrance of the country house in front of which the guests' cars will soon be parked. She scarcely crosses the threshold.

Rapid dissolve to the profile of the girl as she goes up the steps of the hall. In the foreground, a three-quarter profile of the mother, seated in an armchair, silently observing her daughter's arrival.

84. Shot of the young girl, allowing us to see her breast and, in the foreground, her hand resting on the balustrade, sliding over it, with the ring finger bandaged. (Add, if necessary, a close-up of the hand sliding over the balustrade.)

84a. Close-up.

85. Half view, taken from above, of the mother seated in her armchair and still holding in her right hand the book she had been reading. She follows attentively the arrival of her daughter. Brusquely, she asks her: "Is your finger bandaged (86)?" The daughter asks if her father has come home yet. The mother replies affectionately that "He is still at the pharmacy. He will go to his room directly when he comes in to change for the party (87)." When the young girl has almost finished a long speech, her mother, without letting her complete it, interrupts to say, "Hurry up because the people from Majorca will begin to arrive at nine o'clock."

86. Switch to the daughter, who stops when she hears her mother's voice. She looks in the direction of her mother and answers her in a tone of indifference, "Yes, my finger has been sore for over a week." A pause, then, "Father has come in." Scarcely has a shot of the father in his pharmacy shaking a vial of some liquid faded when the girl explains to her mother, "We went out together and there are already six people from Majorca here. The littlest one was singing like the others and had a little mustache. Only the pianist was not there. They advised us to use a Mario-later who plays the piano very well. Six of these musicians will be enough because, with six of them placed close to the microphone, there'll be as much noise as with sixty placed at a distance. It is obvious that a lot of sound is lost in the open air, but we can place the guests close to the orchestra. I had thought . . ." Here the mother interrupts to tell her to go and dress. The young girl obeys and goes quickly up the stairs.

87. Close-up against counters full of vials, bottles, small boxes, etc., of the young girl's father, the Marquis, convulsively shaking a vial. His ring finger—the same one that the young girl had bandaged and that on the poster had disappeared in the hole—stoppers the opening of the bottle. The entire oscillating movement of the hand comes from this finger.

88. Wide-angle view of the hall. The mother, seated, sees her daughter go upstairs. Dissolve to a general view of a bedroom.

89. (This room is the same one which, in the last scenes of the film, the desperate character enters after giving himself a blow

on the head following a love scene.) Shot of the door alone for a few moments, until the young girl comes to open it to enter the room. In the background we see the young girl's bed occupied by a cow. On seeing the animal, the girl goes rapidly toward the bed.

89a. Middle-distance shot of the young girl closing the door. She sees the cow. Reaction.

89b. Shot of the cow stretched out on the bed as calmly as if she were in a stable, as if she were quite used to this. The young girl enters the camera's range and violently orders the cow to go. Raising her arm and pointing as if she were chasing away a dog, she drives the cow from the bed.

90. Shot filmed from behind the bed with the cow in the foreground and the young girl beyond her. The cow gets off the bed. The young girl, still after her, makes her leave the scene by moving left out of the camera's range. The young girl moves around the bed in order to follow the cow.

91. Middle-distance shot of the door to the room, with the cow leaving it at that moment. The young girl follows almost immediately and closes the door. (From this moment on, the sound of the tinkling cowbell persists in the room. Then begins the bedroom-woodland scene, accompanied by music.) Once the door has been closed, the young girl returns to the interior of the room and goes toward the dressing table.

92. Close-up of the dressing table taken at an angle so that one does not see the image reflected in the mirror. The young girl arrives and sits down before it. Her face is very calm, although her glance, as if she were lost in a dream, reflects some inner contemplation of a cherished vision. She looks vaguely, almost automatically, in the mirror and picks up the nail buffer. (These scenes very slow.)

93. Closer shot. The young girl sits facing the dressing table and is photographed head on. She begins to buff her nails with automatic movements which are not, however, continuous; each stroke of the buffer is distinct, and she does not look at what she is doing. After a few strokes, she leaves the buffer on the dressing table. She stares unseeingly at her nails, then looks into the mirror. Her eyes are full of tears. Her crossed hands have been placed on her

breast, near the heart, but again in such an automatic way as to diminish the otherwise theatrical effect of this gesture. (Rapid dissolve.) The young girl follows her amorous dream, nodding her head gently; her forehead is wrinkled slightly and her eyes are brimming with tears. On hearing a dog bark, she gives a little start; her feelings grow more intense. She bites her lips to tie in with the movements of the character in 95.

94. Opening in soft focus. Shot taken from behind the grating of a garden. In the foreground, a dog presses against the grillework; he is barking at someone who must be approaching along the sidewalk. The suspect and the policemen appear on the sidewalk beyond the grille. The expression of the suspect is similar to that of the young girl—that is to say, his eyes, too, are filled with tears and his manacled hands are, like the young girl's, placed over his heart. The suspect tries to stop, looking at the dog with great tenderness (93).

95. Insert of the suspect in the attitude described above. He is biting his lips slightly, to tie in with the same gesture of the girl in 93.

96. Cut to the young girl in the state described above, looking at herself desperately in the mirror (97). Her hair and clothing start to move gently in the wind that comes from the mirror (final shot, 97).

97. Close-up of the mirror, which reflects neither the young girl nor the room but a sunny sky with a few white, oval clouds moving lazily in the west. In the foreground, the dry silhouette of a tree shaken by the wind.

98. Profile shot of the young girl and the mirror, taken in such a way as to show the outdoor scene the mirror reflects. The young girl, her hair still moved by the wind, leans her forehead against the mirror. She holds her face in her hands.

Slow dissolve. After the scene is cut, leave a few feet of blank film. Cut the resulting darkness with a rapid pan in.

❈   ❈   ❈

The feathers continue to fall.

237. Rapid dissolve to an identical field and angle, but this covered with snow. Rising vertical panoramic shot discloses a steep

and immense mountain covered with snow. At the edge of a precipice looms the threatening silhouette of a medieval château. Rapid dissolve to the château in the foreground. Dissolve to façade, with its portals shut, in the foreground.

The feathers, superimposed, still fall.

At the precise moment when the feathers his frantic hands had torn out were covering the ground below the window, the survivors of the Château de Selligny were leaving. To celebrate this most bestial of orgies, four wretches had shut themselves up in the impregnable castle. They were notoriously deep-dyed scoundrels who had no god but lust, no law but depravity, no check but their riotous imaginations—roués without a God, principles, or religion, more steeped in infamy than any criminal you can name. In their eyes, the life of a woman—but what am I saying, a woman?—of *all* women dwelling on the face of the earth was a matter of no more concern than the life of a fly.

They had taken eight marvelous young girls with them to the Château—eight splendid adolescent girls to serve their unspeakable purposes—and, to excite imaginations already corrupted by excess, the four monsters had also brought four depraved women who fueled their criminal lust with lascivious stories.

Now the survivors of these criminal orgies are issuing forth from the Château de Selligny.

The four organizers and leaders. The Duc de Blangis.

238. Close-up. From the portal that opens so slowly that its rusty hinges seem to prevent its swinging wide appears the radiant head of a man wearing a beard and mustache. He is dressed in the fashion of the Hebrews of the first century A.D.

239. Shot taken from a little farther off in order to be able to take in the whole figure of the Duc de Blangis. His eyes are half closed, dazzled as he is by the whiteness of the snow after the long period inside the dark Château. He looks behind him to see if he is being followed, then comes forward.

Two other characters follow, one after the other.

One, his body half dressed in Oriental style (fourth century B.C.), the other dressed as an Arab of the lower classes (sixth century A.D.). After pausing to note the direction the first char-

acter has taken (240, which follows the subtitle), both follow him. The fourth character, who limps, is dressed in the style of a sixteenth-century priest. He takes the same direction as the others. They should appear and move off rapidly.

President Curval and financier Durcet.

240. Torso shot of the leading character near a snow-covered rock, in the attitude of a man waiting for someone in order to move on. The others enter the scene and, without a word, go to stand near the first in order to wait also for whoever is missing.

The one of the four who is missing, Bishop K.

Foreground shot of the door, which has stayed open. The door alone is seen for a moment.

241. A terrified girl of about thirteen appears on the threshold. She is dressed in a loose-fitting gown and with one hand clutches her chest at the spot where one breast is stained with blood (242). She drops down, exhausted, right on the doorsill. The last of the characters comes into camera range, and, picking the young girl up in his arms (242 and following), he returns with her to the Château. A pause in which nothing abnormal happens except that a great, frightful cry comes from the interior. A few moments later, the same unchanging character re-emerges to join the others, moving out of range as a result.

242. Close-up and half-body shot of the young girl, who comes out of the Château, terrified, and of the bishop, who takes her in his arms and enters the Château with her. To be cut into the foregoing in two takes.

243. Snow-white background. Camera in vertical plunging shot. Beaten by the snow and wind, the four unchanging characters move into the camera on the right until they are visible to the waist (the actors should walk up a ramp).

Rapid dissolve to a snow-covered cross, laced with women's hair, cruelly whipped by the wind and whitened by the snow.

NAZARÍN (excerpts from screenplay)

The Sick Child

Nazarín, the priest, compromised because he has given aid to the prostitute Andara, and threatened with arrest for a murder committed in legitimate self-defense, has had to leave the wretched furnished house that sheltered him. He has taken to the open road after having given up his ecclesiastical garb—to the great satisfaction of his superiors—in order not to besmirch "ecclesiastical dignity" by the mendicant's life he must henceforth lead. After his departure, Andara sets fire to the house, then leaves the village in the company of another woman, Beatrice. Nazarín and Andara, both guilty in the eyes of the law of murder and arson, are being sought by the police.

On a road along which he is begging, Nazarín meets Beatrice.

BEATRICE: Oh, Father Nazarín!

NAZARÍN: Why, Beatrice!

BEATRICE: It's a miracle that I ran into you, Father.

NAZARÍN: Why do you say that? The world is small, you know.

BEATRICE: What has happened to bring you to such a state?

NAZARÍN: I've become a beggar.

BEATRICE: You're going around barefoot?

NAZARÍN: I slept last night with the family of some poor people and I gave my shoes to the eldest one. He no longer had any.

BEATRICE: What happened to the rest? Surely, you had something else.

NAZARÍN: A fellow traveler who looked like a pious old priest stole my coat and whatever else I had. Well, what he took wasn't worth much. And what are you doing here?

BEATRICE: I'm going to my sister's. She lost her husband a year ago. Andara lives with us.

NAZARÍN: Dear Lord, why? She had no other place to go! I am glad I met you. God keep you, daughter.

BEATRICE: Come to our house. It's nearby. My sister would be so pleased.

NAZARÍN: I'm sorry, but I have to go beg for a few clothes and something to eat. I will come see you another day.

BEATRICE: Come to the house. My sister has her husband's clothes, she'll give them to you. Help us, Father, help us. Her daughter has been sick for nearly a month and Andara keeps saying, "If only Father Nazarín were near us, he would drive out the child's illness right away." I forgot to tell you that my sister wanted to go to Mexico [City] to bring you back to us.

NAZARÍN: What a ridiculous idea!

BEATRICE: Please, Father. My sister is so unhappy. Do me the kindness of coming to console her.

NAZARÍN: Agreed. I would not refuse a word of consolation or a prayer for her. I'll come, but on condition no one speaks to me of anything else.

They arrive at the house of Beatrice's sister, Josefa. Neighbor women are watching over the child.

JOSEFA: God has sent you to this house, Father! I know you are a real saint.

NAZARÍN: You are talking nonsense. How is the child?

JOSEFA: She is dying, Father Nazarín. If you don't perform a miracle, nothing can save her.

NAZARÍN: Only God and Science can perform miracles of that kind.

BEATRICE: Father, do sit down.

NAZARÍN: Just what is wrong with her?

JOSEFA: She is consumed by fever. I don't know what to do. The day she fell ill, I knew a curse had befallen us because an owl had screeched all night long, and as soon as I went out in the morning three dogs barked, one after the other.

NAZARÍN: Have you had the doctor?

BEATRICE: Yes, Father. He ordered this medicine, and she's already taken two bottles of it.

JOSEFA: Yesterday she was purged, but that didn't help, either. Oh, Father, I don't know which way to turn.

NAZARÍN: Go on doing what the doctor tells you to. Have courage, and keep your faith in God.

A NEIGHBOR: Only a miracle can save her.

BEATRICE: God has already performed one in sending you here, Father.

A NEIGHBOR: And he goes his way barefoot, as did our Lord Jesus Christ!

JOSEFA: Save my child, Father Nazarín, save my child!

NAZARÍN: If I did not know that your grief blinds you, I would not stay here a minute longer. Come, now! How could I succeed where medical science has failed!

JOSEFA: I know you can perform a miracle.

A NEIGHBOR: It's true. I can see in your face that you're a saint! Save her.

ANOTHER NEIGHBOR: Recite the prayers of extreme unction and she will recover.

BEATRICE: For God's sake, Father.

A NEIGHBOR: Perform a miracle. This mother suffers so. Take pity on her. Perform a miracle, for God's sake.

NAZARÍN: Ignorant wretches, don't blaspheme! A miracle? Me?

ANDARA: Yes, yes, a miracle! If you refuse these poor people, it is because you have no wish to help them.

Nazarín turns to Andara.

NAZARÍN: You too, witless woman! What do you take me for? An impostor? Do you think I try to make fools of people? Let no one say another word to me about miracles or I'll think you are making fun of me!

JOSEFA: Oh, take pity on me!

BEATRICE: Yes, take pity on my sister!

ANDARA: You are heartless, Father.

NAZARÍN: Enough, enough! I am not a healer. If God wishes to take this child, it is because He wishes the good of her soul and is trying yours. Let us join together in prayer and seek to resign ourselves. Where is your daughter?

JOSEFA: This way, Father!

Nazarín and the woman approach the child's bed.

NAZARÍN: Of Your goodness, Lord, cure this innocent child. In exchange I offer You my health and my life, and I humbly accept all the calamities, reverses, and trials that may befall a man.

BEATRICE: Help us, God of kindness!

A NEIGHBOR: Help us, Lord, help us!

ANOTHER NEIGHBOR: Flee, demon! Your dwelling is not here!

ANDARA: Withdraw, Satan! You will profit nothing here. On Good Friday, I swear that I will say a thousand times, Jesus! Jesus! Jesus!

A NEIGHBOR: Lord, lean over us that Your hand may protect us!

ANOTHER NEIGHBOR: Help us, Lord, help us!

The women lament and invoke Heaven. One recites the Lord's Prayer. Nazarín prays in silence.

❀

❀   ❀

The next day, Nazarín again meets Beatrice and Andara.

BEATRICE: Father Nazarín, the child is better. Even this morning, it seemed she was dying. Then, all of a sudden, she opened her eyes and asked me for something to eat. I felt her forehead and it was no longer burning. Stay, Father, stay! The news has spread and people are coming to our house to touch the child.

NAZARÍN: Good, good. But you could have told me the news without telling me all this foolishness. Get up and forget this nonsense, I beg you.

ANDARA (*To* BEATRICE): I told you you'd never convince him! It's a miracle, a great miracle, there's no doubt about it!

NAZARÍN: You are both mad! Thank the Good Lord Who has seen fit to grant you His mercy. Farewell.

❀

❀   ❀

Beatrice and Andara follow Nazarín.

NAZARÍN: Where are you two going?

ANDARA: Wherever you go, Father Nazarín.

BEATRICE: We have decided to follow you because we too wish to beg on the high roads.

ANDARA: And become good and holy as you are.

NAZARÍN: Your intentions are excellent, but I admit I would prefer it if you went elsewhere to sanctify yourselves. Do you think I am mad enough to take you along with me? Just imagine that! Decidedly, I have no luck.

The two women have followed Nazarín just the same.

NAZARÍN: Why are you following me?

ANDARA: The road belongs to everyone, doesn't it?

BEATRICE: We wish to do penance and learn from you what is good.

NAZARÍN: I have already told you, if you wish to do penance, do it by yourselves. Let each one stay with his own conscience and in his own solitude!

ANDARA: But how do we annoy you, Father? What ingratitude! We offer him such friendship and he sends us off!

BEATRICE: But if you abandon us, what do you want to become of us?

NAZARÍN: All right, come along. But you must promise to conduct yourselves decently, to be obedient, and above all to leave me in peace.

Nevermore will Beatrice and Andara leave Nazarín.

VIRIDIANA (excerpts from screenplay)

67. *Exterior, the garden. Night. General shot. Dolly.*

Rita draws near the door of the room where she sleeps with her mother. She looks toward the interior, which is plunged in darkness, but she does not dare enter. She goes toward the main building and the household dog, wagging his tail, comes up to her. She pats him, sighing with satisfaction; she seems to have found in

him the protection she was looking for. Quieter now, she pushes the animal by its haunches and goes to sit down on a bench by the doorstep. In the dark courtyard two beams of light clearly shine out from the upper rooms. Rita, leaning forward, looks in the direction of the light.

68. *Interior, living room. Evening.*

Viridiana, seated in the same chair as in the preceding scene, is listening to the first movement of César Franck's Sonata in F together with Don Jaime, who listens inattentively, leaning against the console of the record player. Ramona is seated on a low chair near the little table on which is the coffee service. She is finishing her coffee in small sips. As she brings the cup to her lips, she looks at the young novice. With fear? Or is she waiting?

Viridiana, her back to the camera, holds the empty cup in her hand.

Don Jaime rouses himself from his false torpor. He raises his eyebrows, looks at his niece, then at Ramona. He walks about, and his steps lead him behind Viridiana whom he now observes anxiously.

69. *Close-up. Panoramic.*

Viridiana's right hand, holding the cup and saucer. The pressure of her fingers slacks and what she holds slips to the floor. Don Jaimes holds his breath. He is right behind her. He stops to note her reactions. He looks at Ramona. Then he speaks, in a hesitant voice.

> Don Jaime: You seem very tired. Perhaps you should go to bed.

There is no answer. Virdiana's head leans toward one shoulder. Don Jaime moves slowly forward until he is facing the young girl.

> Don Jaime (*Shaking her gently*): Viridiana! Viridiana!

He receives no answer. Then, walking cautiously, he approaches the record player and stops it.

70. *Exterior, garden. Night.*

Rita pushes the dog so that he'll go away. She has decided to go up to Don Jaime's rooms to look for her mother.

RITA: Run away, now, Lucero!

Without giving the dog another thought, she goes slowly toward the stairs. She isn't very sure of how welcome she'll be upstairs, but she starts to go up little by little.

71. *Interior, corridor. Evening.*

The hallway is lit only by the light that comes from the living room. At the far end, Rita's little silhouette appears as she at last reaches the main floor. She enters the hallway cautiously, heading for the living room where she hears half-muffled voices.

VOICE OF DON JAIME: Help me! Take her legs. . . .
VOICE OF RAMONA: Lift her up a little higher, sir. . . .

There is a pause. Sound of a chair falling.

VOICE OF DON JAIME: Don't think ill of me, Ramona. I just want to keep her near me.

The camera has drawn near Rita. Steps are heard approaching the door, and the little girl runs to hide behind a piece of furniture. From there she observes the scene, frightened.

Don Jaime and the servant arrive from the living room, carrying the body of Viridiana, who seems dead. They go toward Doña Elvira's room, which they enter.

Rita comes out of her hiding place. Spurred by curiosity, she would like to see more, but she is afraid of being caught. She beats a retreat and turning back her head every so often she starts slowly down the stairs.

72. *Interior, Doña Elvira's room. Foreground shot.*

They have just placed the novice's inert body on the bed. Don Jaime makes a sign to Ramona to leave, and she obeys in silence.

Viridiana is still stretched out on her back in the same position. Her hair is in slight disorder, as it was shortly before when she took off the bridal veil. Don Jaime puts it in order again, nervously but with minute artistry. Then he replaces the crown of orange blossoms, crosses her hands on her breast, joins her feet together, arranges the folds of her dress. Stretched out thus, Viridiana looks like a beautiful prostrate statue.

73. *Exterior, garden. Night. General shot.*

The great tree under whose branches little Rita usually plays. We see her drawing near the tree, looking every so often toward the dimly lit window of Doña Elvira's room. After a moment's hesitation, the little girl starts to climb the tree, whose topmost branches are a few yards above the roof of the house.

74. *Crane shot.*

We follow Rita as she climbs. She finally finds a good spot and settles down astride a branch which is about on a level with Doña Elvira's room. From there, she watches with curiosity whatever is going on.

75. *Interior, Doña Elvira's room. Evening. General shot. Middle distant shot. Close-up on dolly.* (From Rita's point of view)

Don Jaime, without taking his eyes off the body of the novice, paces back and forth. He stops for an instant, then goes to sit on the bed. He caresses Viridiana's forehead and hair. He is deeply moved. Then he puts an arm under the young girl's shoulders and lifts her lightly to a sitting position. He bends down and touches her lips with his in a sweet, prolonged kiss.

Suddenly his eyes note the uncurtained window and the night. He carefully lowers Viridiana on the bed and goes toward the window. He closes it and draws the curtains. Then he goes to the door and turns the key.

76. *Exterior, garden. Night. General shot.*

Rita clambers down the tree and jumps to the ground. She sees her mother coming from the farmhouse and runs toward her.

> RAMONA: What are you doing here?
> RITA: Don Jaime was kissing the lady.

Ramona looks at her daughter with a worried expression. Then she realizes how her daughter could have found out. She frowns, annoyed.

> RAMONA: If he's kissing her, that's because she's his niece. Don't I kiss you? You ought to be in bed.
> RITA: A black bull came in the room.
> RAMONA: Shut up, now! I'm going to put you to bed.

She takes the child by the hand and leads her toward the servants' quarters.

77. *Interior, Doña Elvira's room. Evening. Close-up panning to middle-distance shot.*

We see Don Jaime's trembling hands unhooking the false bride's corsage. Her throat and the upper part of her breasts appear, uncovered. This defenseless body, so long desired, is now at his mercy. He is completely overcome.

He places his cheek against Viridiana's breast, feels the delicacy and warmth of her skin. He kisses her, once, twice.

Suddenly he recoils. He straightens up and looks almost with dread at the inert body. He sees the calm, serene expression on the novice's face. Don Jaime passes rapidly at this point from the blind world of instinct to that of conscience. He understands the baseness of his act. At bottom, he is a good and gentle man.

Yet his hands are still stretched out toward her. Suddenly resolved, as if moved by fear of himself, he hurries toward the door, opens it, and goes down the hallway.

78. *Interior, corridor. Evening. General shot.*

We see Don Jaime pass by on his way to his room. He is walking with a rapid and nervous step. He opens his door, enters, and shuts it violently. Absolute silence reigns in the house.

79. *Exterior, landscape. Day. From close-up to general shot. Panoramic.*

The camera ranges from a few ruins still barely lit by the rising sun to a general view of the uncultivated fields of the property. The murmur of a stream is heard.

The mooing of a cow, the cry of birds.

80. *Interior, Doña Elvira's room. Day. Middle-distance shot. Dolly.*

Viridiana is still sleeping an apparently untroubled sleep. She is between the sheets, dressed in a nightgrown. We see an exposed portion of her breast. At the foot of the bed, Ramona is dozing on a chair, keeping watch over the young girl.

The cries of birds continue to be heard from outside.

Viridiana slowly opens her eyes. Absent expression. She runs her

tongue over her lips. A gesture of displeasure. Then her eyes focus on the indistinct silhouette of the servant.

Ramona, aware that Viridiana is awake, draws near. She smiles at her.

VIRIDIANA: I'm thirsty.

Ramona pours her a glass of water from a bottle standing on the little table. Viridiana drinks eagerly.

VIRIDIANA: My head aches.
RAMONA: It will pass. It's nothing.

Viridiana notices her partial nakedness and, embarrassed, covers herself.

VIRIDIANA: What happened to me?
RAMONA: Last evening, you fainted after dinner. The master and I carried you in here.

The novice covers herself up to her chin with the sheet. She is disturbed at having been undressed and put to bed. The servant is aware of this.

RAMONA: I undressed you this morning.
VIRIDIANA: Did I sleep a long time?
Ramona nods her head in assent.
VIRIDIANA: Give me some more water.

The woman pours her another glass of water which she drinks with the same avidity. Steps are heard approaching the room. Viridiana puts down the water glass and withdraws under the sheets.

The door opens and Don Jaime appears. His face and the disarray of his clothes clearly show the sleepless night he has spent. He stands a moment, undecided, motionless in the shadow.

On seeing him, Viridiana wishes to protest but she does not dare. He comes into the room.

DON JAIME: Leave us, Ramona.
VIRIDIANA (*Emphatically*): Don't go!

Don Jaime nods toward the servant and she obeys. She leaves

the room, closing the door behind her. The uncle and niece are face to face.

VIRIDIANA: Uncle, please leave me. I want to get up.

He does not reply. The old man walks, deep in thought, up and down the room, doubtless not knowing how to begin. She insists, irritated.

VIRIDIANA: I must leave.

Don Jaime reacts to this and approaches the bed. He answers firmly.

DON JAIME: No. Now you can no longer leave.

There is a flash of impatience, almost of anger, in the young girl's eyes.

VIRIDIANA: Last evening you promised me never to speak of that again. I beg you, leave me alone now.

Don Jaime, impassive, sits down at the foot of the bed. Viridiana shows signs of beginning to be afraid.

DON JAIME: (*Very calmly, his eyes fixed now on her, now on the clouds one sees passing beyond the branches of the great tree*): What can be further apart than an old man like me, withdrawn from the world, and a young girl like you, promised to God? And yet . . .

The young girl, annoyed, sits almost upright.

DON JAIME: For you, I've forgotten everything, even the passion that kept me alive so many years—everything!

Viridiana would gladly get up and make him leave the room, but her state of undress prevents her.

DON JAIME: I was mad. I thought that you would agree to marry me, but naturally you refused. And now the day has come for you to leave.

She looks at him, wondering how the conversation will end. Don Jaime straightens up and looks at her fixedly.

DON JAIME (*Coldly*): I had to force your will. (*A pause*) That was the only way I could hold you in my arms.

Viridiana is overwhelmed. Increasing anxiety. She stammers.

> VIRIDIANA: You lie!
>
> DON JAIME: No, it's true. (*Speaking very distinctly*) Last night, while you were sleeping, you were mine.

She stares at him with horrified eyes. She cannot believe what he is saying. She feels a cold sweat break out on her forehead.

Don Jaime starts to walk up and down before her once more, now fixing her with his eyes, now looking obstinately at the ground.

> DON JAIME: Now you can no longer return to your convent. You are no longer the girl who left it a few days ago. You must stay with me forever.

He stops. There is a note of supplication in his voice.

> DON JAIME: Everything I have will be yours, and if you prefer not to marry me, if you prefer to go on living as we have until now, I will resign myself to it as long as you stay near me. . . .

It takes a visible effort for Viridiana to understand her uncle's words. The shock has been so great that she scarcely reacts. Her distress arouses compassion in Don Jaime.

> DON JAIME: Think it over. Don't hurry. Think it over.

> VIRIDIANA (*As if waking from a nightmare, almost screaming*): Go away! Leave me alone!

She looks at him with hatred and disgust. Don Jaime is startled by this. He hesitates. He is about to say something, but decides against it. Finally he goes toward the door. He feels Viridiana's blazing eyes fixed on him. He goes out, destroyed, his head lowered.

81. *Interior, corridor. Day. Middle-distance shot.*

We see Don Jaime, uncertain and torn by doubt, leave the room. The idea that he has committed an unpardonable error in lying to Viridiana is working within him.

82. *Interior, Don Jaime's room. Day. Middle-distance shot.*

Ramona is waiting for him and Don Jaime passes her without even seeing her. He sits down heavily on the edge of his bed. Ramona slowly approaches him. She dares ask him:

RAMONA: What did you say to her, sir?

He raises his head toward her.

DON JAIME: How she looked at me, Ramona! Now she hates me. I made a grave mistake. She's going away, she's going away for good.

RAMONA (*Tonelessly*): Speak to her again. Tell her seriously how things are.

DON JAIME: What would be the good? She would look at me again like that. . . . I can't do it. You go. Perhaps she'll listen to you. Try to convince her.

RAMONA: But sir, what am I to tell her?

DON JAIME: Tell her I lied to her, tell her I did her no harm.

Ramona looks at him open-mouthed, incredulous.

DON JAIME (*With deep sincerity*): I intended to, Ramona. But I came to my senses in time. I spent the night thinking, thinking. . . . And then I lied to her so that she would not dare go back there.

He gets up and takes Ramona by the arm.

DON JAIME: Go to her. Explain.

He almost pushes her toward the door. She goes hesitantly, reluctantly.

83. *Interior, Doña Elvira's room. Day. Middle-distance shot.*

Viridiana is finishing getting dressed and is closing her valise at the moment the door opens and the servant timidly shows her face. Viridiana's eyes are full of tears. We see Ramona hesitate a moment, then turn and go rapidly toward Don Jaime's room.

84. *Interior, Don Jaime's room. Day. General shot.*

Don Jaime in the foreground, leaning against his bed. Ramona appears in the doorway.

RAMONA: Come right away, sir; she's going.

Don Jaime straightens up at once. He stares at the servant, then moves rapidly toward the door and goes out.

85. *Interior, Doña Elvira's room. Day. General shot.*
Viridiana places her veil on her head, takes up her valise, and is starting to go when her uncle enters the room. He stands in her way. The young girl's eyes are still tearful.

VIRIDIANA: Let me pass!
DON JAIME: Before you go, you must hear me out.
VIRIDIANA (*Bitterly*): I have heard you quite enough. Let me leave.

In lieu of an answer, the old man locks the door and puts the key in his pocket.
Viridiana backs away from him and puts down her valise. She is no longer afraid. She can scarcely feel any emotion other than rage mingled with disgust.
Don Jaime drops into a chair.

DON JAIME: Everything I told you before is a lie. I said it so that you would not go away. I harmed you only in my thoughts. I can't bear to have you leave hating me.

He looks at her in supplication.

DON JAIME: Tell me that you believe me and I will let you go.
VIRIDIANA: You disgust me . . . even if what you say is true.
DON JAIME (*In a quieter voice*): Then . . . can't you forgive me?

The look the young girl gives him completes Don Jaime's destruction. He gets up painfully, more stooped than ever. Perhaps he wishes to inspire at least a ray of pity in his niece. But she remains impassive. He goes toward the door with faltering steps, puts the key in the lock, and opens it. Without looking at him, she hurries out.

86. *Interior, corridor. Day. General shot.*

We see the novice coming from the far end of the corridor toward the camera. Ramona timidly raises her head to watch her pass. Don Jaime's silhouette is shown dimly against the shadows of the room the young girl has just left. Viridiana passes in front of the camera and we hear her hurried steps on the stairs. Ramona runs to meet Don Jaime.

87. *Interior, Doña Elvira's room. Day. General shot.*

Don Jaime, seen from behind, is looking down from the balcony. Ramona enters, overcome by what has been happening. When Don Jaime hears her steps, he turns around. His expression is not what we might have expected. He seems peaceful enough, without the least trace of sorrow. He seems almost to be smiling. Once what he has so dreaded has come to pass, he finds the courage he had simulated before.

The servant stops, eyes downcast, a few steps away from him, not daring to look at him. Don Jaime draws near her.

> DON JAIME: You believe me, don't you?
> RAMONA: Yes, sir.

She says it in a low voice, absolutely lacking in conviction. Don Jaime is immediately aware of this. He smiles and lightly taps her.

> DON JAIME: Don't lie. You don't believe me, either.
> RAMONA (*Looking for an excuse*): It's because—everything is so out of the ordinary, sir.

Don Jaime nods in commiseration.

> DON JAIME: It's all right, my girl. It's all right.

He goes toward the hall. Ramona goes to the bed, strips it and examines the sheets, trying to discover the truth.

88. *Exterior, garden. Day. Close-up.*

Moncho, the manservant, has just finished hitching up the carriage.

A few yards away, Viridiana waits, seated on a stone bench, her back to the camera, her valise nearby.

Rita is playing *diabolo* beside her. The kind of toy Don Jaime has given the child shows what sort of person he is—certainly, "of another age."

RITA: Look how high I can throw it!

Viridiana does not even turn to look. Rita, to attract her attention, picks up the *diabolo,* which did not fall along the string as it should have. She whirls it about and then puts it back in place with the aid of one of the sticks.

RITA: Look! You can't do that!

As the young girl continues to sit lost in thought, Rita grows discouraged and tries to interest Moncho.

RITA: See how high I can throw it!

As usual, he answers her irritably.

MONCHO: Leave me in peace!

Rita keeps on playing, disregarding Moncho's rebuff.

MONCHO (*To Viridiana*): Whenever you're ready . . .

The novice straightens up and goes toward the carriage.

89. *General shot.*

Pan in from behind to a middle-distance focus. Don Jaime is watching his niece's departure from the interior of his room, near the balcony. Downstairs, we see Viridiana approaching the carriage. The little girl says something to her. Viridiana gets in the carriage, and Moncho whips up the horse. The little girl waves goodbye. Then she starts to run after the carriage.

90. *Interior, living room. Day. Middle-distance shot.*

Don Jaime sadly watches the carriage drive away. But he soon pulls himself together and his face takes on an expression of calm, almost of indifference.

He goes toward a worktable in the corner of the room and sits down at it. He passes a hand over his forehead. On the table, all his work tools are in disorder. Certainly months have passed since Don Jaime has touched his work. Meticulously, he starts to put things to rights again. He draws a finger over the table top to see

whether there is any dust. He looks at his finger. Seeing that it is clean, he smiles, thinking of Ramona's care.

At last, he takes a piece of paper and a pen and starts to write with great concentration. The camera is right over him.

91. *Exterior, town street. Day. General panoramic shot.*
The bus that runs daily to the station is just about to arrive. It turns a corner of the street.

92. *Exterior, town square. Day. Middle-distance shot. Shot in depth. Crane.*
The bus enters the square and pulls up at the bus stop. A group of people wait for it there. A few of them carry packages. The driver gets down. When the camera pans in, we find Viridiana among the travelers. The driver clambers onto the roof to tie on the luggage that is handed him. Viridiana passes up her valise.

93. *From general to middle-distance shot.*
At the other end of the street, a man approaches on a mule. He goes toward the town hall which faces on the same square. Near the main entrance to the building, the mayor is talking with two or three people. The man on muleback gets down and approaches the group. He says something. The reaction of the mayor and his interlocutors is strange. They surround the man, as if asking him for explanations, and they all talk for a moment. Then the mayor turns his head toward where the bus has stopped. He rushes toward it.

94. *Dolly traveling forward.*
Two travelers have just gotten into the bus and Viridiana is about to do likewise when the mayor arrives, almost running, and stops her by taking hold of her sleeve.

> THE MAYOR: Excuse me, miss, but you can't leave.
> VIRIDIANA (*Surprised*): Why not?
> THE MAYOR (*Looking at her fixedly, scratches his neck. It costs him an effort to speak out.*): Something bad has happened. Come.

Viridiana neither protests nor questions.

Dissolve.

95. *Exterior, garden of the house. Day. General shot.*

Two cars stop before the entrance. The mayor, accompanied by Viridiana and the men who were with him in the square, gets out of one of them. From the other car two police officers and a man in civilian dress emerge. They all enter the property. We cannot distinguish Viridiana's expression amid this little throng.

96. *Exterior, garden. Day. Middle-distance.*

Ramona is seated under the great tree that little Rita had climbed. She wipes her tears with a handkerchief. Swing to catch Rita farther off, her eyes wide open and fixed on the tree. A little farther away, a group of four or five peasants, men and women, exchange comments in low tones.

97. *General shot. Dolly.*

The mayor's group comes toward the camera. Among them is Viridiana. A few yards from the tree, they stop and force themselves to look up at something among the branches. Some of them show horror, others, curiosity.

98. The great tree. In the midst of the foliage, we see a hanging body.

99. *Middle-distance shot. Viridiana.*

The young girl has just glimpsed it, too. She closes her eyes and covers them with her hand, not to see the frightful sight.

100. *Close-up.*

The branch on which Don Jaime's body hangs. We do not see the body itself which is suspended below, outside the frame. But we see the knot that attaches the rope to the tree. The rope has a wooden handle. It is little Rita's jumping rope.

Dissolve to darkness.

4. CRITICISM

UN CHIEN ANDALOU: A Poet's Lucidity

BY JACQUES B. BRUNIUS

[*Cahiers d'Art*, June 1929]

Luis Buñuel is possessed by a fury that knows no hope, and by a drive to demolish barriers that serve no purpose; he has that vital energy that compels all true men to face the most agonizing problems of life. From metamorphosis to metamorphosis, from double vision to double vision, he forces us unremittingly to confront him and ourselves. People make much of the imaginative and grotesque elements in his work. (It is a fact that the same people are always wrong in the same ways.) With Buñuel, however, it is not a question of inventiveness but rather of that lucidity proper to poets which allows them to strip away appearances, to reveal dramatic points of contact between the mind and the outside world, to discover unusual but true combinations. Events are linked in a way that recalls the absurd yet implacable necessity of the dream until the association of idea and image seems automatic.

L'AGE D'OR: Divine Orgy

BY HENRY MILLER

[*The New Review*, Paris, 1931]

I know nothing of his precursors. I see him standing alone on a Himalayan peak, reeling among the clouds. I see him with lightning in both hands, dancing at the edge of a precipice. Far below I see the crowd growling, roaring, cursing first and then praying, I hear the rumble of the flood, I know that everything

181

will be destroyed—man, his creations, his myths, his gods . . . everything.

Like an entomologist, he has studied what we call love in order to expose beneath the ideology, the mythology, the platitudes, and phraseologies, the complete and bloody machinery of sex. He distinguishes for us the blind metabolisms, the secret poisons, the mechanistic reflexes, the distillations of the glands, the entire plexus of forces which unite love and death in life—a biochemical metempsychosis in which the individual perishes so that the species may survive.

What matter then that the Republic of France is erased, that capitalism is decapitated, that the religion of Christianity is scotched? Violence, destruction, vilification, blasphemy, perversion, etc., etc. In a creation of the first order, in a sweep that is not less epic than the Homeric legends or the saga of the Nibelungs, these elements are essential. The whole fabric of society is torn apart, layer by layer, tissue by tissue; one is given to see the nerves and blood vessels, the inner organs, the articulation of the skeletal structure.

Is this art? Who cares a damn? The fools will call it surrealism and go away chewing definitions. Of course it is not art. Art is a shibboleth. It is a divine orgy in the face of the divinest orgy known to man: sex. It begins with scorpions who duel among the rocks and ends with a cross—a cross garlanded with beautiful female scalps. There is a Duc de Blangis who is the devil disguised as Jesus Christ, and there are other personages, well known to the astute, who are admittedly neither this nor that. There are the chief protagonists—Lya Lys and Gaston Modot. There is a blind man who is mistreated, there is a dog which is kicked in the stomach, there is a boy who is wantonly shot by his father, there is an old dowager who is slapped in the face, there is a clown in priestly raiment who plays the fiddle, there is . . .

Is it necessary to say that there are scenes in this film which have never before been dreamed of? There is a scene, for example, which by a supreme tour de force achieves the miracle of divine poetry. I quote from the program:

It is useless to add that one of the culminating points of the film's purity seems to us to be crystallized in the vision of the heroine in the toilet; here [the director's] imaginative power enables him to sublimate a situation that would normally be in questionable taste into a poetic episode of the purest nobility and solitude.

There is a *paso doble* which carries the film to a shatteringly triumphant conclusion. Novel in its simplicity, it would be unthought of except by a mad Lear. Following the orgasms of Wagner, it sounds the death knell of the race. Man is doomed to perish; he has betrayed his instincts, he has sacrificed everything to intelligence. While he regards himself as the crown of creation, Buñuel exhibits him as mineral, vegetable, animal—as an organic entity composed of all the elements, as a contradictory entity, as temple and madhouse, as flower and insect, as beast and clown.

Man's intelligence vastly surpasses his physical parts; it submerges them; it levies impossible and absurd demands on them, whence the railroad, the telegraph, the microscope, and all else that multiplies the potency of organs rendered ineffectual by the exigencies of the brain, our master. It has also required more of the sexual organs than they were able to offer, and to satisfy these demands a mode of conduct was devised whereby dreams and flowers are strewn over the bed of love.

What has man done with his instincts? Denied them. The summations of all his laws, his codes, his principles, his moralities, his totems and taboos, what does it yield? Sterility. Death. Annihilation. There are among the lower forms of life beings who lie joined in coition for weeks at a time; there are creatures who, apparently denied what one might call sexual organs, nevertheless derive from mere contact an ecstasy beyond all power of imagination; there are, among certain species, such maladjustments of the physical organs of reproduction that the act of coition, when accomplished, becomes nothing short of a miracle. Below man life flourishes with a prodigal virulence. The goal is reproduction, perpetuation; death is an incident. The host moves on; the individual perishes. In the supreme stage of the drama, so strong at

times is the instinct that the male offers himself not only as fecundating power but as alimentation.

Says Anatole France: "I would have fashioned men and women not after the great apes, as they actually are, but in the image of insects, which, living first as caterpillars, are transformed into butterflies and throughout life have no concern other than to love and to be beautiful. I would have had youth come at the close of human life. In their last metamorphosis, certain insects have wings but no stomach. They are reborn in this refined form to love for the space of an hour and then to die."

The plight of civilized man is a foul plight. He is singing his swan song without the joy of swanhood. He has been sold out by his intelligence. Manacled, strangled, and mangled by his own symbology. Mired in his art, suffocated by his religion, paralyzed by his wisdom. That which he glorifies is not life, since he has lost the rhythm of life, but death. What he worships is decay and putrefaction. His institutions are bankrupt, his brain is diseased. The whole organism of society is infected. Man himself is a disease. In every great city of the civilized world there are savants who lecture on "The Death of the Moon," "Man Before Birth," "Ignorance," "There Is an Afterlife," "The Reflex Cure," "The Fountain of Youth," "Rejuvenation by Blood Transfusion," "The Future Can Be Foretold," "The Interpretation of Dreams," "Freud and Infancy," "Man after Death."

They call Buñuel everything: traitor, anarchist, pervert, defamer, iconoclast. But lunatic they do not call him. It is true, it is lunacy he portrays, but it is not his lunacy. This stinking chaos which for a brief hour or so amalgamates under his wand, this is the lunacy of civilization, the record of man's achievement after ten thousand years of refinement.

The country which hisses him off the boards is the very flower of culture, the grand republic of intelligence and sterility. France, which produces nothing but ideas, France, which has raised l'amour to an art, France represents humanity; beside her the Italians are rabbits, fecund but of a lower order; Germany is the insect world, baffling in its organization, incomprehensible in its cruelty, its love; America is not a land, even, but a sea of neuters,

a spawn of onanists—impregnating blindly, without joy, without feeling.

It is a pity that we have become so refined. We should revert to cannibalism. We are unable any longer to bear the sight of grinning skulls in the agonized composure of death. Before it has even grown cold, we take the decapitated head of a pig or a lamb and blow it up by compressed air. We demand that when things are brought forward on the platter, they shall make the saliva flow.

Attila, Caesar, Napoleon—did they inquire the age, the sex, the nationality of the slain? So Buñuel, handling the raw materials, does not inquire too closely, does not hesitate in the fervid lust of creation to pierce, to shatter, to lance, to decimate. He is the first man who has taken the medium of the screen and used it to the fullest. He shows what hitherto has been denied us, not to shock but to convince.

His violence is a catharsis. There is not a touch of depravity in it. His curses are more pure than all the hymns of the Christian church. If he utilizes the music of Wagner, it is only because his ears are attuned to its potent blasphemy. He is deceived by nothing—not even by the bogus charms of art.

They should take Buñuel and crucify him, or at least burn him at the stake. He deserves the greatest reward that man can bestow upon man.

L'AGE D'OR: Total Love

BY ANDRÉ BRETON

[*L'Amour Fou*, Gallimard, 1937]

To this day, *L'Age d'Or* remains a unique effort to exalt total love, as I conceive it to be;* and the violent reactions which the Paris showings aroused have only strengthened my sense of the film's incomparable value. Love, in all that it can mean to two human

* No longer the only one, but one of two such efforts, for I have since seen that other prodigious film, that triumph of surrealist thought, *Peter Ibbetson*. —A.B.

beings—something absolutely confined to them, isolating them from the rest of the world—has never been shown with such freedom and quiet audacity. Neither stupidity nor hypocrisy nor rigid custom will be able to suppress this work by darkening the screen that shows a man and a woman forcing the world which is ranged against them to witness the spectacle of ideal love. In such a love there flourishes a genuine "golden age" totally at odds with the age of mud through which Europe is stumbling; it is an age inexhaustibly rich in *future* possibilities. I have always applauded Buñuel and Dali for having chosen to stress this.

THE TRADITION OF A FIERCE AND PASSIONAL ART
BY OCTAVIO PAZ

[at the Cannes Festival, April 4, 1951]

Un Chien Andalou (1928) and *L'Age d'Or* (1931) marked poetry's first aggressively deliberate invasion of the art of the cinema. The union of film image and poetic image might seem shocking, even subversive. Indeed, it was. The subversive nature of Buñuel's early films consisted entirely in this: the conventional phantoms—social, moral, and artistic—of which our "reality" is composed were no sooner lightly brushed by the hand of poetry than they fell into dust. Over these ruins a new reality arose, the reality of man and of men's desires. Buñuel demonstrated that a chained man need only shut his eyes to make the world explode. His films, then, are more than a fierce attack on so-called "reality." They are the revelation of another reality that is enslaved by modern civilization. The man of *L'Age d'Or* slumbers in every one of us and is only waiting for a sign—the sign of love—to awaken. As André Breton has said, this film is one of the rare attempts in modern art to bare the terrible face of a love that is free.

Shortly afterward, Buñuel filmed *Las Hurdes*, a documentary which is also in its way a masterpiece. In *Las Hurdes* the poet hides and is silent, so that reality may speak out alone and in its

own language. If the theme of Buñuel's surrealist films is man's struggle against a reality that mutilates and smothers him, the theme of *Las Hurdes* is the brutalizing triumph of that same reality. Thus this great documentary comes as a necessary complement to his earlier works. It explains and justifies them. Here, by different paths Buñuel pursues his unremitting war with—or more exactly, against—reality. His own realism is allied, in the highest Spanish tradition, to that of Goya, Quevedo, the picaresque novels, Valle-Inclán, Picasso. The battle is waged in a hand-to-hand combat that gives no quarter. Reality emerges from this encounter stripped to the bone. His art is in no way related to the sentimental or aesthetic description that customarily passes as being realistic. Quite the contrary. All Buñuel's work provokes in us a liberating eruption of something secret and precious, something dreadful and pure, something that our concept of reality ordinarily shrouds from our sight.

Whether he uses the device of dream or poetry or cinematic narrative, Buñuel the poet penetrates man's profoundest being and reaches the most unexpressed, deep-lying areas of his inner self. His hell. And his heaven . . .

If, on one hand, *Los Olvidados* represents a high point of artistic maturity, on the other it testifies to a more complete and total despair. The threshold of the dream seems eternally barred, and only that of the blood stands open. The film is a synthesis of the best of Buñuel's previous work and at the same time is a new point of departure. He does not deny any part of the great experience of his youth, but he has been made more aware of changes wrought by the passing of time—changes that have only made the reality prefigured in his first films even more dense—and he has constructed a work whose action unfolds, as precise as a machine, as hallucinatory as a dream, as implacable as the silent downward flow of lava. *Los Olvidados* has a social theme: juvenile delinquency. The initial situation in the scenario was taken from police records. The characters are alive, or could be. They are our contemporaries. They are the age of our own children. But *Los Olvidados* is more than a realistic film. Dream, desire, horror, delirium, chance, the night portion of life, all find in it their due

place. The weight of the "reality" of which Buñuel makes us aware is so atrocious that we are tempted to believe it impossible to endure. And so it is. Reality is not to be endured. That is why man kills and dies, loves and creates, in turn.

The physical and human limits within which the drama takes place could not be more circumscribed: the life and death of some children, caught within the four walls of their solitude, and thrown like so much fodder to their fate. The city, with all that it implies of human solidarity, turns its back on their little hovels. The modern city does turn its back, morally and physically, on its children. What we call civilization is for them a wall, a huge NO for them to stumble against. These are Mexican children, but they could be of any country, living in the outskirts of any large city. In one sense they no more live in Mexico than anywhere else. They are *los olvidados*—the forgotten ones—inhabitants of those great wastelands that the modern city breeds around it. Theirs is a world closed in upon itself, a world where all action is circular, and where every step they take forces them toward the point they started from. No one is able to escape the presence of others, no one is able to get outside himself except via the blind alley of death. Other worlds do exist in which chance opens doors. Here it closes them.

The continual presence of chance invests *Los Olvidados* with a special meaning that prevents our confusing it with fate. The chance that governs the actions of the heroes of the story is presented as an absolute necessity, and yet one that "could have been avoided." (Why not call it, as in tragedy, by its right name—destiny?) Stripped of its supernatural attributes, the ancient fatality marches on. Today ours is a psychological and social fatality, or, to use the current catchword, our new intellectual fetish—a historical necessity. But it is not enough that society or history or circumstance be hostile to the heroes of the story for catastrophe to fall upon them; its determinants must coincide with the will of those who are involved. Pedro fights against chance and the bad luck that Jaibo represents for him. When finally he faces these forces squarely and submits to them, he transforms chance into destiny. He dies, but he has made his death his own. The tragedy

derives from the impact between human awareness and external fatality. Buñuel has rediscovered a fundamental ambiguity: without human complicity destiny cannot be fully achieved and tragedy is impossible. Fatality dons the mask of liberty, and liberty that of destiny.

Los Olvidados is not a documentary. Still less is it a film with a thesis, or a propaganda or a moralizing film. But if no preachments tarnish its admirable objectivity, it would be libelous to suggest, on the other hand, that it is a film in which only artistic values (always suspect, in any case) are important.

The film of Buñuel and Figueroa is as remote from realism, whether social, psychological, or uplifting, as it is from aestheticism. It takes its place in the tradition of a passional and fierce art, a contained and delirious art reminiscent of Goya and of the Mexican engraver Posada, who of all plastic artists have unquestionably pushed the grotesque to its furthest extremes. Cold lava, volcanic frost . . .

The moral value of *Los Olvidados* has nothing to do with propaganda. When art is free it does bear witness; it is conscience. Buñuel and Figueroa's work is proof of what the creative talent and conscience of two artists can accomplish when nothing but their own freedom constrains or enslaves them.

THE DEPTHS OF REALITY
BY ANDRÉ BAZIN

[*Esprit,* January 15, 1952]*

We apprehend the grandeur of *Los Olvidados* immediately we sense that the film involves no reference to moral absolutes. There is no trace of Manichaeism in the characters; their destinies cross like daggers but it is only a passing conjunction; their guilt is fortuitous. Of course, speaking on the psychological and moral level, one could say of Pedro that at bottom he is good, that he has a fundamental purity; he is the only one to walk through this

* Also in *Qu'est-ce que le Cinéma,* Vol. III, Éd. du Cerf, 1961.

sea of mud and not be spattered or contaminated by it. Yet Jaibo, the bad character—perverse, sadistic, cruel, and disloyal—does not inspire repugnance so much as a kind of horror that is by no means incompatible with love. He makes one think of Genêt's heroes—with this difference: the author of *Le Miracle de la Rose* deals with an inversion of values that we do not find in Buñuel's film. These children are beautiful not because they are good or bad but because they are children, in crime as in death. Pedro is the childhood brother of the Jaibo who betrays and kills him, and although each becomes what his childhood makes of him, they are equal in death. Their dreams are the measures of their destiny. Buñuel performs the utterly remarkable feat of recreating two dreams in the worst tradition of Freudo-Hollywoodian surrealism that nevertheless leave us tremulous with horror and pity. Pedro has run away because his mother would not give him the meat sandwich he wanted. He dreams that his mother gets up in the middle of the night to offer him a whole quarter of raw, bloody meat but that Jaibo, who is hidden under the bed, reaches out and snatches it away. We can never forget this piece of meat that palpitates like a dying polyp as the mother offers it with her Madonnalike smile. Nor will we forget the miserable, mangy mongrel trotting through the last night of Jaibo's conscious life and dying in some shadowy nowhere, its forehead crowned in blood. I am inclined to think that Buñuel has given us the only contemporary aesthetic expression of Freudianism. The surrealists made use of it too self-consciously, and we do not respond when symbols are deliberately injected into their paintings. By contrast, *Un Chien Andalou, L'Age d'Or,* and *Los Olvidados* present us with psychoanalytical situations in all their profound and irrefutable veracity. Whatever the plastic form (in this instance, highly debatable) Buñuel gives to the dream, his images have the pulse and the burning affectivity of dreams. The thick blood of the unconscious circulates through them and, as if it were flowing from an open artery, inundates us. . . .

It is absurd to reproach Buñuel with having a perverse taste for cruelty. True, he does seem to choose his situations for the sake of their paroxysmal horror. What is more frightful than a child

stoning a blind man, unless it be a blind man revenging himself
on a child? The body of Pedro, who has been murdered by Jaibo,
is tossed on a dimly outlined garbage heap, among dead cats and
empty cans, and the people who get rid of him by throwing him
there are among the very few who care about him, no less—a
little girl and her father. But the cruelty is not Buñuel's; he merely
reveals the cruelty that rages in the world. If he selects the most
excruciating examples, that is because the real problem is not to
know that happiness also exists but to know to what lengths the
cruelty of creation can go. This intention was already evident in
the documentary on the Hurdanos. It did not matter whether
those wretched people were or were not truly representative of
the poverty of the Spanish peasant (unquestionably, they were),
but that they were representative of human misery. Thus, between Paris and Madrid it was possible to take the measure of
human decadence. Not in Tibet nor in Alaska nor in South Africa,
but right down in the Pyrenees, men like you and me, heirs of the
same civilization, members of the same race, had become cretinous
goatherds, subsisting on green cherries, too brutish to brush the
flies from their own faces. It does not matter that they are an exception; what matters is that such a thing can be. Buñuel's surrealism is nothing more than his concern to get to the bottom of
reality; what matter if we lose our breath as the diver loses his
head when, in his cumbersome suit, he cannot feel the ocean floor
under his foot. The dreamlike nature of *Un Chien Andalou* is a
plunge into the depths of the human soul, just as *Terre sans Pain*
[*Las Hurdes*] and *Los Olvidados* are an exploration of man in
society.

Buñuel's so-called cruelty is entirely objective; it is nothing
more than lucidity and nothing less than pessimism. If pity is
absent from his aesthetic canon, that is because compassion everywhere enfolds his work. At least this is true of *Los Olvidados*, for
it seems to me that, in this particular respect, we must recognize
a development in Buñuel beyond *Terre sans Pain*. In its objectivity, the documentary on the Hurdanos was not without a certain
cynical note of complaisance; the withholding of pity became an
aesthetic provocation. *Los Olvidados*, on the other hand, is a film

of love and demands love. Nothing can be more unlike existential-
ist pessimism than Buñuel's cruelty. Because it evades nothing,
concedes nothing, dares with surgical obscenity to make an in-
cision in the corpus of reality, his cruelty can rediscover man in
all his grandeur and can, by a kind of Pascalian dialectic, compel
us to love and admiration. Paradoxically, the predominant feeling
to emerge from both films is an impression of incorruptible human
dignity. In *Terre sans Pain* a mother sits motionless, holding the
body of her dead child in her lap, and the face of this peasant
woman, numbed by poverty and grief, has all the beauty of a
Spanish *Pietà*, in which nobility and harmony are compounded.
Similarly, in *Los Olvidados* even the most hideous faces never fail
to be in the image of man. This presence of the beautiful in the
dreadful (it is not merely the beauty *of* the dreadful), this endur-
ance of human nobility in the midst of decadence, dialectically reverse cruelty into an act of love and compassion. It explains why
the public does not respond to *Los Olvidados* with either sadistic
complicity or pharisiacal indignation.

A SOLITARY POWER
BY MICHEL PICCOLI*

As a film maker Buñuel is literally out of this world, for he has
never been able to understand the restrictions imposed by the
economics of film making. Either that, or he pretends that they
don't exist. He simply does not know how to navigate in this
world. He makes no claim to be fighting a given kind of film; he
is simply a poet who acknowledges certain exigencies proper to a
man of his day.

Then there is his respect and love for all that is human. He
does not like to meet the world socially, but he is humble before
the single human being. He does not indulge in sentimentality,
but is always most lucid. His astuteness, his humor, and his
great courtesy are astonishing; they help him to live. This is rare.

* A young actor who played in *La Mort en Ce Jardin*.

I have seen him turn quickly aside to avoid someone whose work he admires but who in his personal life "has behaved badly." He neither wanted to shake hands with the man nor to affront him by refusing to do so. He cannot bear people who make him uncomfortable. He crawls back into his shell. Gives up. He is a solitary power, yet he is no superman; when something disgusts him, he lets go, becomes artful, diabolic, and so achieves his purpose. He has a horror of the sensational. His films, furthermore, do not aim at being scandalous. They are, like him, profoundly and powerfully human. Do people realize his respect for the faith of others? For example, I saw him once unable to endure a mocking joke at the expense of a Mexican. Personally, he has been and always will be disturbed by Christianity. This forms one part of his argumentation. Could he possibly be alone? He sees men suffer for a faith that offers them no salvation. His work is not introspective; it proclaims, it demonstrates what he sees. And with what candor and clarity! Both from the point of view of plot and pure technique. That's what surprises and "shocks" us. His work is always moving and modest, although one tends to forget this.

It has been a privilege to know Buñuel and to have been a means of interpreting in his films the magnitude of his heart as well as his ideas.

THE EASY JOB

BY OSCAR DANCIGERS

What I think of Buñuel is very simple: he is a great director. To me, directing is the easiest part of film work and anybody can do it—even the job of make-up is more difficult. I believe Buñuel himself thinks so. But that is why it is hard, even almost impossible, to be a good director. Buñuel—with a handful of other film makers —is remarkably good.

I consider, and so does Buñuel, that the genuine director is at the same time a writer, an author. Buñuel is that kind. The essential part of the film is finished for him before the actual directing

begins. That is only a simple matter of execution, and he is most impatient to get it finished and done with as fast as possible, which explains the astounding speed of his shooting.

Once the film is finished, Buñuel becomes once more what he is above all else—a simple man who loves life simply. In his quiet personal life, he is the middle-class father of a family, surrounded by few but very close friends, modest and economical in his way of life. He loves to eat, drink, hunt—all pleasures of a man firmly rooted in the earth. In his own life there is not the slightest trace of the unusual.

CHRONOLOGY

1926   Assistant director under Jean Epstein of *Mauprat.*

1927   Assistant director under Mario Nalpas and Etiévant of *La Sirène des Tropiques* (*The Siren of the Tropics*).

1928   Assistant director under Jean Epstein of *La Chute de la Maison Usher* (*The Fall of the House of Usher*).

1928   Director of *Un Chien Andalou* (*An Andalusian Dog*).
Nationality: French. Producers: Luis Buñuel and Salvador Dali. Scenario: Luis Buñuel and Salvador Dali. Music: Excerpts from *Tristan und Isolde,* by Richard Wagner. Cast: Pierre Batcheff, Simone Mareuil, Jaime Miravilles, Salvador Dali, Luis Buñuel.

1930   Director of *L'Age d'Or* (*The Golden Age*).
Nationality: French. Producer: Viscount Charles de Noailles. Scenario: Luis Buñuel. Music: Excerpts from works by Beethoven and Wagner. Original music: Georges van Parys. Cast: Gaston Modot, Lya Lys, Max Ernst, Pierre Prévert.

1930   Brief trip to Hollywood.

1932   Director of *Las Hurdes* (also called *Tierra sin Pan*—in English, *Land Without Bread* and also *Unpromised Land*).
Nationality: Spanish. Producer: Ramón Acín. Assistant directors: Pierre Unik, Sanchez Ventura. Commentary: Pierre Unik. Photography: Eli Lotar. Music: Excerpts from Brahms's Fourth Symphony.

1933-1935   Dubbing for Paramount in Paris.

1935   Supervisor of co-productions and dubbing for Warner Brothers in Spain.

1935 Executive producer of *Don Quintín el Amargo* (*Don Quintín, the Bitter One*).
Nationality: Spanish. Producers: Filmofono. Director: Luis Marquina.

1935 Executive producer of *La Hija de Juan Simón* (*Juan Simón's Daughter*).
Nationality: Spanish. Producers: Filmofono. Director: José Luis Saenz de Heredia.

1936 Executive producer of *Quién Me Quiere a Mí?* (*Who Loves Me?*).
Nationality: Spanish. Producers: Filmofono. Director: José Luis Saenz de Heredia.

1936 Executive producer of *Centinela! Alerta!* (*Sentinel, On Guard!*).
Nationality: Spanish. Producers: Filmofono. Director: Jean Grémillon.

1937 Collaborator on the documentary series *España Leal en Armor* (*Loyalist Spain in Arms*).

1937 In France: Supervisor of *Espagne 39* (*Spain 39*) of J.-P. Le Chanois.

1938 In the United States: Director of documentaries for the Museum of Modern Art, New York City.

1940 Supervisor of Spanish-language versions at M-G-M.

1942 Director of documentaries on the American Army.

1944-1946 Dubbing for Warner Brothers.

1946 In France: Uncompleted project, *La Casa de Bernarda Alba* (*Bernarda Alba's House*), after the play by Federico García Lorca.

1947 In Mexico: Employed by the producer Oscar Dancigers. Director of *Gran Casino*, formerly titled, *En el Viejo Tampico*.
Nationality: Mexican. Producer: Anahuac (Oscar Dancigers). Scenario: Michel Weber. Adaptation: Mauricio Magdaleno. Dialogue: Javier Mateos. Photography: Jack Draper. Music: Manuel Esperón. Scenery: Javier Torres. Editing: Gloria Schoeman. Cast: Libertad Lamarque, Jorge Negrete, Mercedes Barba, Agustín Isunza.

1949 Director of *El Gran Calavera* (*The Great Madcap*).
Nationality: Mexican. Producer: Ultramar Films (Oscar Dancigers). Scenario: Raquel Rojas and Luis Alcoriza, after a comedy by Adolfo Torrado. Photography: Ezequiel Carrasco. Music:

Manuel Esperón. Scenery: Luis Moya and Dario Cabanas. Cast: Fernando Soler, Rosario Granados, Rubén Rojo, Andrés Soler, Maruja Grifell, Gustavo Rojo, Luis Alcoriza.

1950 Director of *Los Olvidados* (*The Young and the Damned*). Nationality: Mexican. Producer: Ultramar Films (Oscar Dancigers). Scenario: Luis Buñuel and Luis Alcoriza. Photography: Gabriel Figueroa. Music: Rodolfo Halffter, on themes of Gustavo Pitaluga. Scenery: Edward Fitzgerald. Sound: José B. Carles. Editing: Carlos Savage. Cast: Estela Inda, Miguel Inclán, Alfonso Mejía, Roberto Cobo, Hector López Portillo, Salvador Quiros, Victor Manuel Mendoza.
Prize for the best direction, Cannes Film Festival, 1951. International Critics' Prize.

1950 Director of *Susana* (formerly titled *Demonio y Carne—The Devil and the Flesh*). Nationality: Mexican. Producer: Internacional Cinematográfica (Oscar Dancigers). Scenario: Jaime Salvador, after a story by Manuel Reachi. Photography: José Órtiz Ramos. Music: Raul Lavista. Scenery: Gunter Gerzso. Sound: Nicolas de la Rosa. Cast: Rosita Quintana, Fernando Soler, Victor Manuel Mendoza, Matilde Palau.

1951 Director of *La Hija del Engaño* (*Daughter of Deceit*), a remake of *Don Quintín el Amargo*. Nationality: Mexican. Producer: Ultramar Films (Oscar Dancigers. Scenario: Raquel Rojas and Luis Alcoriza, after a story by Carlos Arniches. Photography: José Órtiz Ramos. Music: Manuel Esperón. Scenery: Edward Fitzgerald. Sound: Eduardo Arjona. Cast: Fernando Soler, Alicia Caro, Rubén Rojo, Nacho Contra, Fernando Soto, Lily Aclemar.

1951 Director of *Una Mujer sin Amor* (*A Woman Without Love*). Nationality: Mexican. Producer: Internacional Cinematográfica (Oscar Dancigers). Scenario: Jaime Salvador, after the novel *Pierre et Jean* by Guy de Maupassant. Photography: Raul Martínez Solares. Music: Raul Lavista. Cast: Rosario Granados, Julio Villareal, Tito Junco, Joaquín Cordero.

1951 Director of *Subida al Cielo* (*Ascent to Heaven*). Nationality: Mexican. Producer: Isla (Manuel Altolaguirre). Scenario: Manuel Altolaguirre. Photography: Alex Phillips. Music: Gustavo Pittaluga. Scenery: Edward Fitzgerald and José Rodriguez Granada. Cast: Lilia Prado, Carmen González, Esteban Márquez, Luis Aceves Castañeda, Manuel Dondo, Roberto Cobo.

Prize for the best *avant-garde* film, Cannes Film Festival, 1952.

1952 Director of *El Bruto* (*The Brute*).
Nationality: Mexican. Producer: Internacional Cinematográfica (Oscar Dancigers). Scenario: Luis Buñuel and Luis Alcoriza. Photography: Agustín Jiménez. Music: Raul Lavista. Scenery: Gunter Gerzso. Editing: Jorge Bustos. Cast: Pedro Armendariz, Katy Jurado, Rosita Arenas, Andrés Soler.

1952 Director of *Robinson Crusoe*.
Nationality: Mexican. Producers: Oscar Dancigers and Henry F. Ehrlich (for Ultramar). Scenario: Luis Buñuel and Philip Roll, after the novel by Daniel Defoe. Photography (Pathé color): Alex Phillips. Music: Anthony Colins. Scenery: Edward Fitzgerald. Editing: Carlos Savage and Alberto Valenzuela. Cast: Dan O'Herlihy, Jaime Fernandez, Felipe de Alba, Chel López, Emilio Garibay.

1952 Director of *El* (*He*).
Nationality: Mexican. Producer: Oscar Dancigers (for Nacional Film). Scenario: Luis Buñuel and Luis Alcoriza, after a novel by Mercedes Pinto. Photography: Gabriel Figueroa. Music: Luis Hernandez Breton. Scenery: Edward Fitzgerald. Editing: Carlos Savage. Cast: Arturo de Cordova, Delia Garces, Luis Beristain, Aurora Walker, M. Baena.

1953 Director of *Abismos de Pasión* (*Wuthering Heights*).
Nationality: Mexican. Producer: Tepeyac. Scenario: Luis Buñuel, after the novel by Emily Brontë. Photography: Agustín Jiménez. Music: Raul Lavista; excerpts from Wagner. Scenery: Edward Fitzgerald. Sound: E. Argona. Cast: Irasema Dilian, Jorge Mistral, Lilia Prado, Ernesto Alonso, Luis Acevas Castañeda, Francisco Requeira.

1953 Director of *La Ilusión Viaja en Tranvía* (*Illusion Travels by Streetcar*).
Nationality: Mexican. Producers: Clasa Films Mundiales. Scenario: Mauricio de la Serna and José Revueltas. Photography: Raul Martínez Solares. Music: Luis Hernandez Breton. Scenery: Edward Fitzgerald. Cast: Lilia Prado, Carlos Navarro, Agustín Isunza, Miguel Manzano, Javier de la Parra, Guillermo Bravo Sosa, Felipe Montojo.

1954 Director of *El Rio y la Muerte* (*The River and Death*).
Nationality: Mexican. Producers: Armando Ozive Alba for Clasa Films Mundiales. Scenario: Luis Buñuel and Luis Alcoriza, after

the novel by Miguel Alvarez Acosta. Photography: Raul Martínez Solares. Music: Raul Lavista. Scenery: Edward Fitzgerald and Gunter Gerzso. Editing: Jorge Bustos. Cast: Columba Dominguez, Miguel Torruco, Joaquín Cordero, Jaime Fernandez, Victor Alcover.

1955 Director of *Ensayo de un Crimen* (*Practice of a Crime;* also called *La Vie Criminelle d'Archibald de la Cruz, The Life of Crime of Archibald de la Cruz*).
Nationality: Mexican. Producer: Alfonso Patino Gómez for Alianza Cinematográfica. Scenario: Luis Buñuel and Eduardo Ugarte, after a story by Rodolfo Usigli. Photography: Agustín Jiménez. Music: Jesús Bracho and José Pérez. Cast: Ernesto Alonso, Miroslava, Rita Macedo, Ariadna Welter, Rodolfo Landa, Andrés Palma, Carlos Riquelme, J. María Linares Rivas, Leonor Llansas.
In France: Director of *Celà S'Appelle l'Aurore* (*That Is Called Dawn*).
Nationality: Franco-Italian. Producers: Les Films Marceau (Paris) and Laetitia Films (Rome). Scenario: Luis Buñuel and Jean Ferry, after the novel by Emmanuel Roblès. Dialogue: Jean Ferry. Assistant directors: Marcel Camus and Jacques Deray. Photography: Robert Le Febvre. Music: Joseph Kosma. Scenery: Max Douy. Sound: Antoine Petitjean. Editing: Marguerite Renoir. Cast: Georges Marchal, Lucia Bosè, G. Esposito, Nelly Borgeaud, Julien Bertheau, Jean-Jacques Delbo, Gaston Modot, Henri Nassiet, Simone Paris.

1956 In Mexico: Director of *La Mort en Ce Jardin* (*Death in This Garden*).
Nationality: Franco-Mexican. Producers: Dismage (Paris) and Tepevac, Oscar Dancigers (Mexico). Scenario: Luis Buñuel, Luis Alcoriza and Raymond Queneau, after the novel by José-André Lacour. Dialogue: Raymond Queneau and Gabriel Arout. Photography (Eastman color): Jorge Stahl, Jr. Music: Paul Misraki. Scenery: Edward Fitzgerald. Sound: José Pérez. Editing: Marguerite Renoir. Cast: Simone Signoret, Georges Marchal, Charles Vanel, Michel Piccoli, Michèle Girardon, Tito Junco.

1956 In France: Uncompleted project, *La Femme et le Pantin,* after the novel by Pierre Louÿs.

1957 In France: Uncompleted project, *Thérèse Étienne,* after a novel by John Knittel.

1958 In Mexico: Director of *Nazarín.*

Nationality: Mexican. Producer: Manuel Barbachano Ponce. Scenario: Luis Buñuel and Julio Alejandro, after the novel by Benito Pérez Galdós. Supervision of Dialogue: Emilio Carballido. Photography: Gabriel Figueroa. Editing: Carlos Savage. Production Consultant: Carlos Velo. Cast: Francisco Rabal, Marga López, Rita Macedo, Ignacio López Tarso, Noe Murayama, Jesús Fernandez.

Special Jury Prize, Cannes Film Festival, 1959.

1959 In Mexico: Director of *La Fièvre Monte à El Pao* (*The Fever Reaches El Pao*).
Nationality: Franco-Mexican. Producers: C.I.C.C., Cité Films, Indus Films, Terra Films, Cormoran Films (Paris) and Filmex (Mexico). Scenario: Luis Buñuel, Luis Alcoriza, Charles Dora, and Louis Sapin, after the novel by Henry Castillou. Dialogue: Louis Sapin. Photography: Gabriel Figueroa. Music: Paul Misraki. Sound: William Robert Sivel. Cast: Gérard Philippe, María Félix, Jean Servais, Raoul Dantes, M.-A. Ferriz, Domingo Soler, Victor Junco, Roberto Candedo.

1959 In France: Uncompleted project, *Beau Clown,* after the novel by Berthe Grimault.

1960 In Mexico: Director of *La Jeune Fille* (*The Young One*).
Nationality: Mexican. Producer: Georges P. Werker for Producciones Olmeca. Scenario: Luis Buñuel and H. B. Addis, after the novel *Travellin' Man* by Peter Matthiessen. Photography: Gabriel Figueroa. Music: Jesús Zarzosa. Sound: James L. Fields, José P. Carles, and Galdino Samperio. Editing: Carlos Savage. Artistic Direction: Jesús Bracho. Cast: Zachary Scott, Bernie Hamilton, Kay Meersman, Crahan Denton, Claudio Brook.

Special mention *hors concours,* Cannes Film Festival, 1960.

1961 In Spain: Director of *Viridiana.*
Nationality: Spanish. Producer: Gustavo Alatriste for Uninci and Films 59. Scenario: Luis Buñuel. Photography: José A. Agayo. Scenery: Francisco Canet. Editing: Pedro del Rey. Executive Producer: Ricardo Muñoz Suay. Cast: Silvia Pinal, Francisco Rabal, Fernando Rey, Margarita Lozano, Victoria Zinny, Teresa Rabal.

Co-winner of the Grand Prix, Cannes Film Festival, 1961. Winner of the Prix de l'Humeur Noir pour le Cinéma, 1961.

1962 In Mexico: Director of *El Angel Exterminador* (*The Exterminating Angel*).
Nationality: Mexican. Screenplay by Luis Buñuel from a story

by Luis Alcoriza and Luis Buñuel. Director of Photography: Gabriel Figueroa. Sound Engineer: José B. Carles. Art Director: Jesús Bracho. Cast: Silvia Pinal, Nadia Haro Oliva, Patricia Moran, Augusto Benedico, Luis Beristain, Tito Junco, Jacqueline Andere, García Alvarez, Claudio Brooks, Javier Loya, Ofelia Guilmaín, José Baviera.

NOTE: In preparing this chronology, we have relied extensively on the one published in *Cinema Universitario*, the magazine published by the Ciné-Club of Salamanca (No. 12, July 1960); that listing was compiled under the supervision of Luis Buñuel. We have also obtained information from the filmography by Freddy Buache which was published in *Premier Plan*, No. 13. Last, and above all, Luis Buñuel has kindly supplied us with an exact chronology of his productions and thus allowed us to correct several points in the information furnished by these two sources.

BIBLIOGRAPHY

NOTE: Selections in this volume are not included.

ENGLISH

Aubry, Daniel, and Lacor, J. M., "Luis Buñuel." *Film Quarterly*, Vol. XII, No. 2 (Winter 1958), pp. 7-9.

Bachmann, Gideon, "The Films of Luis Buñuel." *Cinemages*, Vol. I, No. 1 (1955), pp. 10-17.

Barcia, J. Rubia, "Luis Buñuel's *Los Olvidados*." *Quarterly of Film, Radio, and Television*, Vol. VII, No. 4 (Summer 1953), pp. 392-401.

Bellow, Saul, "Buñuel's Unsparing Vision." *Horizon*, Vol. V, No. 2 (November 1962), pp. 110-12.

Buñuel, Luis, "Buñuel on Buñuel." A letter to *Films in Review*. *Films in Review*, Vol. VI, No. 8 (October 1955), pp. 424-25.

———, "Cinema: An Instrument of Poetry." *Theatre Arts*, Vol. XLVI, No. 7 (July 1962), pp. 18-19.

———, "Notes on the Making of *Un Chien Andalou*." In *Art in Cinema*, published by Art in Cinema Society, San Francisco Museum of Art (1947), pp. 29-30.

———, "On *Viridiana*." *Film Culture*, No. 24 (Spring 1962), pp. 74-75.

———, "Out of a Cinema Credo." *The New York Times*, Section 2 (March 18, 1962), pp. 29-30.

———, "Reply to a Questionnaire on the Film Maker and the Audience." In *Film: Book I*, ed. Robert Hughes, New York, Grove Press, Inc., 1959, pp. 40-41.

———, "A Statement." *Film Culture*, No. 21 (Summer 1960), pp. 41-42.

——— and Dali, Salvador, "*Un Chien Andalou*, a Scenario." Includes a synopsis of *L'Age d'Or*, with comments. In *Surrealism*, by Julien Levy, New York, The Black Sun Press, 1936, pp. 64-74.

Cine Club de Zaragoza, Discussion of *Tierra sin Pan*. Program of Session 209 (January 11, 1957).

Dali, Salvador, "Comments on the Making of *L'Age d'Or.*" *Cinemages*, Vol. I, No. 1 (1955), pp. 27-29.

———, "Comments on the Making of *Un Chien Andalou.*" *Cinemages*, Vol. I, No. 1 (1955), pp. 25-27.

García-Abrines, Luis, "Rebirth of Buñuel." Yale French Studies, No. 17, *The Art of the Cinema* (Summer 1956), pp. 55-66.

Knight, Arthur, "The Films of Luis Buñuel." *Saturday Review* (July 1954), p. 27.

Miller, Henry, "The Golden Age." In *The Cosmological Eye*, New York, New Directions, 1939. Also reprinted in *Film: An Anthology*, ed. Daniel Talbot, New York, Simon and Schuster, 1959, pp. 498-509; and in *Cinemages* (retitled "Age of Gold"), Vol. I, No. 1 (1955), pp. 18-25.

Paz, Octavio, "*Nazarín.*" *Film Culture*, No. 21 (Summer 1960), pp. 60-62.

Richardson, Tony, "The Films of Luis Buñuel." *Sight and Sound* (January-March 1954).

Riera, Emilio G., "The Eternal Rebellion of Luis Buñuel." *Film Culture*, No. 21 (Summer 1960), pp. 42-58.

———, "The Films of Luis Buñuel." *Film Culture*, No. 21 (Summer 1960), pp. 58-60.

———, "*Viridiana.*" *Film Culture*, No. 24 (Spring 1962), pp. 76, 81-82.

"Talk with the Director." *Newsweek*, No. 59 (March 26, 1962), pp. 96-97.

Young, Vernon, "Buñuel and Antonioni." *The Hudson Review*, Vol. XV, No. 2 (Summer 1962), pp. 274-81.

FRENCH AND SPANISH

Agel, Henri, "Au Coeur de l'Insolite: Luis Buñuel." In *Miroirs de l'Insolite dans le Cinéma Français*, Éd. du Cerf, 1958.

———, "Luis Buñuel." In Les Grands Cinéastes, Éd. Universitaires, 1959.

Almendros, Néstor, "Buñuel, Hombre de Cine." *Cuadernos*, Paris (July 1963). *Cuadernos* is a Spanish language magazine distributed in Latin America; it is banned in Spain.

Aranda, J. F., "Buñuel, Espagnol." *Cinéma 57* (Christmas 1957).

———, various articles in *Cinema Universitario*, Nos. 10, 12, Salamanca (1960).

Aranda, L., "Buñuel." *Cinema Universitario*, No. 4, Salamanca (1959).

Arout, Gabriel, "En Travaillant avec Buñuel." *Cahiers du Cinéma* (October 1956).

Buache, Freddy, "Luis Buñuel." *Premier Plan*, No. 13 (1960).

Buñuel, Luis, *Un Chien Andalou. Revue du Cinéma*, No. 5 (November 15, 1929); also in *Anthologie du Cinéma* by Marcel Lapierre, La

Nouvelle Édition, 1946. (These are in addition to authorized version in this book, originally published in *La Révolution Surréaliste*.)

———, "El Cine, Instrumento de Poesía." *Cinema Universitario*, No. 12, Salamanca (1960).

———, *Viridiana*. The screenplay, with an introduction by Georges Sadoul. Paris, Domaine Cinéma, InterSpectacles, 1962.

Buñuel, Luis, special issues of magazines devoted to: *Image et Son*, No. 157 (December 1962; *La Méthode*, No. 7 (January 1962); *Positif*, No. 10 ("Le Cinéma Mexicain-Buñuel," 1954) and No. 42 (November 1961).

Dali, Salvador, *La Vie Secrète de Salvador Dali*. Éd. La Table Ronde, 1952.

Études Cinématographiques, Nos. 20, 21 (Winter 1962-63).

Hell, Henri, "Buñuel, le Plus Violent des Metteurs en Scène . . ." *Arts* (June 9, 1954).

Kast, Pierre, "Une Fonction de Constat. Notes sur l'Oeuvre de Buñuel." *Cahiers du Cinéma* (December 1951).

——— and others, "A la Recherche de Buñuel . . ." *Cahiers du Cinéma* (December 1951).

Kyrou, Ado, *Amour, Érotisme et Cinéma*. Éd. Le Terrain Vague, 1957.

———, *Le Surréalisme au Cinéma*. Éd. Arcanes, 1953.

Laclos, Michel, "L'Homme a Scandale du Cinéma." *Télémagazine*, No. 313 (October 1961).

Laude, André, "La Vatican contre Buñuel." *France-Observateur*, No. 585 (July 1961).

Mardore, Michel. "L'Anvers des Fiorettis." *Cahiers du Cinéma*, No. 127 (January 1962).

Mauriac, Claude, "Luis Buñuel." In *L'Amour du Cinema*, Éd. Albin Michel, 1954.

Michel, Manuel, "L'Homme sans Chaînes." *Cinéma 61* (January 1961).

Pena, José, and Salachas, Gilbert, "Luis Buñuel." *Téléciné*, No. 106 (August-September 1962).

Philippe, Claude-Jean, "Luis Buñuel du *Chien Andalou* à *Nazarín*." *Télérama* (December 18, 1960).

Pornon, Charles, *La Rêve et la Fantastique dans le Cinéma Français*. Éd. La Nef de Paris, 1959.

Rambaud, Charles, "Luis Buñuel," *L'Écran et la Vie*, No. 10 (December 1962).

Robles, Emmanuel, "À Mexico avec Buñuel," *Cahiers du Cinéma* (February 1956).

Sadoul, Georges, "Lettre à Pierre Kast," *Cahiers du Cinéma* (January 1952).

———, "Mon Ami Buñuel," *L'Écran Français*.

Seguin, Louis, "En Attendant Buñuel." *Positif*, No. 47 (July 1962).

Tranchant, François, "Dossier Luis Buñuel." *Image et Son* (December 1958).

Trebouta, Jacques, *Luis Buñuel, Sa Vie, Son Oeuvre en Espagne et en France* (unpublished). Institut des Hautes Études Cinématographiques.

————, "Une Scandaleuse Tendresse." *Cinéma 56* (December 1956).

Individual Films—Comment and Review (arranged chronologically)

UN CHIEN ANDALOU

Brunius, Jacques B., "*Un Chien Andalou*." *Revue du Cinéma* (October 15, 1929).

Aron, Robert, "Filmes de Révolte." *Revue du Cinéma* (November 15, 1929).

Brunius, Jacques B., "*Un Chien Andalou; L'Age d'Or*." In *En Marge du Cinéma Français*, Éd. Arcanes, 1947.

Piazza, François, "Considerations psychoanalytiques sur *Un Chien Andalou*." *Psyché* (January-February 1949).

Audiberti, "Billet 1." *Cahiers du Cinéma* (July 1954).

Mondragon, "Comment J'ai Compris *Un Chien Andalou*." *Cinéclub*, No. 8-9 (May-June 1959).

Mauriac, Claude, "Buñuel et la Liberté de Création." *Le Figaro Littéraire* (January 7, 1961).

L'AGE D'OR

Dreyfus, J.-P., review of film. *Revue du Cinéma* (December 1930).

Spitz, Jacques, "La Poésie du Cinéma." *Revue du Cinéma* (January 1, 1931).

Chavance, Louis, "Les Influences de *L'Age d'Or*." *Revue du Cinéma* (February 1, 1931).

Kyrou, Ado, critique of film. *L'Age du Cinéma*, No. 4-5 (1951).

Miller, Henry, "*L'Age d'Or* Vu par Henry Miller." *Philm* (March 1954).

LOS OLVIDADOS

Paz, Octavio, review of film. "*L'Age du Cinéma*, No. 3 (June-July 1951).

Sadoul, Georges, "Cruauté, Tendresse, Pitié." *Les Lettres Françaises* (November 22, 1951).

Doniol-Valcroze, J., "Par Dela la Victime." *Cahiers du Cinéma* (December 1951).

Lo Duca, "Le Film Justifie les Moyens." *Cahiers du Cinéma* (December 1951).

Chardere, Bernard, review of film. *Positif*, No. 1 (1952).

Mauriac, Claude, "Buñuel et la Liberté de Création." *Le Figaro Littéraire* (January 7, 1961).

SUBIDA AL CIELO

Bolduc, Albert, review of film. *Positif*, No. 4 (1952).
Doniol-Valcroze, Jacques, "La Foi Qui Sauve." *Cahiers du Cinéma* (June 1952).
Dorsday, Michel, "Soleils de Buñuel." *Cahiers du Cinéma* (February 1953).

SUSANA

Dorsday, Michel, "Soleils de Buñuel." *Cahiers du Cinéma* (February 1953).

EL BRUTO

Dorsday, Michel, review of film. *Cahiers du Cinéma* (November 1953).

EL

Kyrou, Ado, review of film. *Bizarre*, No. 1 (1953).
Collective article. *Positif*, No. 10 (1954).
Cornaire, Pierre, "À Propos de *El*." *Philm* (March 1954).
Dorsday, Michel, "Ou Révolutionnaire ou Moraliste." *Cahiers du Cinéma* (July 1954).
Doniol-Valcroze, Jacques, "Post-scriptum sur *El*." *Cahiers du Cinéma* (July 1954).

ROBINSON CRUSOE

Doniol-Valcroze, Jacques, "Fiers Comme des Hommes." *Cahiers du Cinéma* (August-September 1954).

LA VIE CRIMINELLE D'ARCHIBALD DE LA CRUZ (French title of *Ensayo de un Crimen*)

Demonsablon, P., review of film. *Cahiers du Cinéma* (November 1957).
Trebouta, Jacques, review of film. *Cinéma 57* (November 1957).
Silberman, J.-C., critique of film. *L'Écran* (January 1958).
Seguin, Louis, review of film. *Positif* (February 1958).

CELA S'APPELLE L'AURORE

Labarthe, André S., "Seul le Cristal." *Cahiers du Cinéma* (June 1956).
Sadoul, Georges, "Hommage à Buñuel." *Les Lettres Françaises* (May 17, 1956).
"L. S.," critique of film. *Positif* (June-July 1956).
Piece in *Image et Son*, No. 101 (April 1957).

Borde, Raymond, review of film. *Carré Rouge,* No. 4 (January-February 1958), Lausanne.

LA MORT EN CE JARDIN

Sadoul, Georges, critique of film. *Les Lettres Françaises* (September 27, 1956).

Moullet, Luc, critique of film. *Cahiers du Cinéma* (November 1956).

Kyrou, Ado, critique of film. *Positif* (December 1956).

Untitled piece in *Image et Son,* No. 108 (January 1958).

NAZARÍN

Aranda, J. F., "La Passion selon Buñuel." *Cahiers du Cinéma* (March 1959).

Olivar, A., "Nazarín y la Polémica y Luis Buñuel." *Linterna Mágica,* Program of the 12th session, Salamanca (April 1962).

Dubreuilh, Simone, "*Nazarín* de Luis Buñuel, l'Envers du *Journal d'un Curé de Campagne.*" *La Cinématographie Française* (May 11, 1959).

Lachize, Samuel, "Encore un Film à Controverse." *L'Humanité* (May 12, 1959).

Baroncelli, Jean de, "Le Soleil et Buñuel Font Monter la Température du Festival de Cannes." *Le Monde* (May 13, 1959).

Flipo, R. P., "Propos sur *Nazarín:* La Gloire de Dieu, C'est l'Homme Vivant." *Rendez-vous de Cannes. La Cinématographie Française* (May 14, 1959).

Paz, Octavio, "Dans la Grande Tradition des Fous Espagnols." *Les Lettres Françaises* (November 24, 1959).

Benayoun, Robert, "*Nazarín,* ou les Points sur les *i.*" *Positif* (November 1959).

Kyrou, Ado, and others, "*Nazarín.*" *Positif* (April 1960).

Gilson, René, "L'Évangile selon Saint Luis." *France-Observateur* (December 1, 1960).

Baroncelli, Jean de, "*Nazarín.*" *Le Monde* (December 3, 1960).

Mauriac, Claude, "Buñuel d'Hier et d'Aujourd'hui." *Le Figaro Littéraire* (December 3, 1960).

Jeander, "*Nazarín.*" *Libération* (December 3, 1960).

Domarchi, Jean, "*Nazarín,* ou Eros contre le Christ." *Arts* (December 7, 1960).

Sadoul, Georges, "Un Nouveau Don Quichotte." *Les Lettres Françaises* (December 8, 1960).

Aub, Max, "Galdós et *Nazarín.*" *Les Lettres Françaises* (December 15, 1960).

Labarthe, André S. "Un Désespoir Actif." *Cahiers du Cinéma* (January 1961).

LA FIEVRE MONTE À EL PAO

Reviews of film by Jean de Baroncelli, *Le Monde* (January 8, 1960); Jacqueline Michel, *Le Parisien Libéré* (January 8, 1960); Michel Aubriant, *Paris-Presse* (January 9, 1960); Jacques Doniol-Valcroze, *France-Observateur* (January 14, 1960); Bruno Gay-Lussac, *L'Express* (January 14, 1960); Gerard Gozlan, *Positif* (May 1960).

Mauriac, Claude, "Un Buñuel sans Maléfice." *Le Figaro Littéraire* (January 16, 1960).

Sengissen, Paule, "Un Essai Politique Qui Emprunte la Trame du Mélodrame." *Radio, Cinéma, Télévision* (January 17, 1960).

LA JEUNE FILLE

Fabre, Jacqueline, "Buñuel sans Bavure." *Libération* (May 7, 1960).

———, "Un Candidat Sérieux à la Palme d'Or." *Le Parisien Libéré* (May 7, 1960).

Sadoul, Georges, "La Jeune Fille." *Les Lettres Françaises* (May 12, 1960).

Douchet, Jean, "Une Oeuvre de Tendresse Humaine." *Arts* (July 5, 1961).

Baby, Yvonne, "*La Jeune Fille.*" *Le Monde* (July 12, 1961).

Jeander, "*La Jeune Fille.*" *Libération* (July 17, 1961).

VIRIDIANA

Michel, Jacqueline, "Un Film Espagnol Risque de Bouleverser le Palmarès." *Le Parisien Libéré* (May 18, 1961).

Fabre, Jacqueline, "Buñuel et Son Crucifix a Cran d'Arrêt." *Libération* (May 18, 1961).

Baroncelli, Jean de, "Buñuel en Liberté." *Le Monde* (May 19, 1961).

Labarthe, André S., "Le Festival au Jour le Jour." *France-Observateur* (May 25, 1961).

Mauriac, Claude, "Du Soufflet au Geste de Bénir." *Le Figaro Littéraire* (June 10, 1961).

Le Fevre, Raymond, "*Viridiana.*" *Image et Son,* No. 152 (June 1962).

EL ANGEL EXTERMINADOR

Erice, Victor, "El Angel Exterminador." *Nuestro Cine,* No. 11 (May 1962).

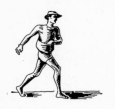